Sports Fundamentals Series

RACQUETBALL
Fundamentals

Jim Winterton

Human Kinetics

Library of Congress Cataloging-in-Publication Data

Racquetball fundamentals / Human Kinetics with Jim Winterton.
    p. cm. -- (Sports fundamentals series)
  ISBN 0-7360-5233-X (softcover)
  1. Racquetball. I. Winterton, Jim. II. Human Kinetics (Organization) III. Series.
  GV1003.34.R316 2004
  796.343--dc22

2004007992

ISBN: 0-7360-5233-X

The Web addresses cited in this text were current as of April 2, 2004 unless otherwise noted.

Developmental Editor: Susanna Blalock; **Assistant Editor:** Cory Weber; **Copyeditor:** Annette Pierce; **Proofreader:** Sue Fetters; **Graphic Designer:** Robert Reuther; **Graphic Artist:** Sandra Meier; **Photo Manager:** Dan Wendt; **Cover Designer:** Keith Blomberg; **Photographer (cover):** Dan Wendt; **Photographers (interior):** Dan Wendt and Terry Wild; **Art Manager:** Kareema McLendon; **Illustrator:** Kareema McLendon; **Printer:** United Graphics

Human Kinetics books are available at special discounts for bulk purchase. Special editions or book excerpts can also be created to specification. For details, contact the Special Sales Manager at Human Kinetics.

Printed in the United States of America

10 9 8 7 6 5 4 3 2 1

Human Kinetics
Web site: www.HumanKinetics.com

United States: Human Kinetics
P.O. Box 5076
Champaign, IL 61825-5076
800-747-4457
e-mail: humank@hkusa.com

Canada: Human Kinetics
475 Devonshire Road Unit 100
Windsor, ON N8Y 2L5
800-465-7301 (in Canada only)
e-mail: orders@hkcanada.com

Europe: Human Kinetics
107 Bradford Road
Stanningley
Leeds LS28 6AT, United Kingdom
+44 (0) 113 255 5665
e-mail: hk@hkeurope.com

Australia: Human Kinetics
57A Price Avenue
Lower Mitcham, South Australia 5062
08 8277 1555
e-mail: liaw@hkaustralia.com

New Zealand: Human Kinetics
Division of Sports Distributors NZ Ltd.
P.O. Box 300 226 Albany
North Shore City
Auckland
0064 9 448 1207
e-mail: blairc@hknewz.com

Welcome to Sports Fundamentals

The Sports Fundamentals Series uses a learn-by-doing approach to teach those who want to play, not just read. Clear concise instructions and illustrations make it easy to become more proficient in the game or activity, allowing readers to participate quickly and have more fun.

Between the covers, this book contains rock-solid information, precise instructions, and clear photos and illustrations that immerse readers in the sport. Each chapter covering the sport's fundamentals is divided into four major sections:

- You Can Do It!: Jump right into the game or activity with a clear explanation of how to perform an essential skill or tactic.
- More to Choose and Use: Find out more about the skill or learn exciting alternatives.
- Take It to the Court: Apply the new skill in a game situation.
- Give It a Go: Use drills and game-like activities to develop skills by doing and gauge learning and performance with self-tests.

No more sitting on the sidelines! The Sports Fundamentals Series gets you right into the game. Apply the techniques and tactics as they are learned, and have fun—win or lose!

Contents

Introduction

Welcome to racquetball, the greatest game on Earth. This game was first played in the early 1950s and was invented by Joe Sobek in Greenwich, Connecticut. Since that time the game has grown. Today more than 10 million people play worldwide. One of the reasons for the sport's popularity is its simplicity. All you need to start is a racket, a ball, a few accessories, and a racquetball court. As shown in figure 1, the game is played on an indoor court 20 feet (6 meters) wide and 20 feet (6 meters) high. The length of this indoor rectangle is 40 feet (12 meters).

Modern-era racquetball rackets are light with big hitting surfaces. Old rackets usually had four and one-quarter inch (10.8 cm) grips. Today's racket grips are generally smaller, usually three and seven-eighths inches (9.8 cm) or smaller. As the racket's hitting surface increased, the handle circumference decreased. Those who have played tennis may find larger grips more comfortable, but most new racquetball players prefer a smaller grip. The smaller grip sizes allow the racket head to get around on the ball faster, allowing you to hit the ball harder.

Most of the rackets today are made of a combination of materials. Rackets are made from materials with fancy names such as titanium and Kevlar and from materials engineered in various combinations. These modern materials reduce vibrations through the

1 **The racquetball court.**

handle, resulting in less stress on your arm. The bottom line is this: If the racket feels good when you play, then play with it. A starter racket in a low price range is appropriate for beginners. Then after playing for a while, you will have a better idea about which racket to graduate to. Most racquetball clubs rent demo rackets so that you can play a few games with them to see if you like them. As a safety measure, all rackets should have a tether on the bottom. The tether should be slid around your wrist when playing or practicing. Without the tether, the racket could cause serious injury if it were to slip out of your hand.

Many common racket sports injuries are caused by overusing the racket. Tendinitis, bursitis, and other soft-tissue injuries are the result of poor technique and sometimes poor equipment. You will sustain fewer overuse injuries if you use a newer racket made of forgiving materials with a larger sweet spot in the racket head. The larger string surface and the larger hitting area reduce the vibrations transferred to your wrist, arm, and shoulders. The lighter and more firm the racket, the easier it will be to handle throughout a match. All of these factors add to less stress on the body and fewer injuries. Of course, as with any sport, be sure to ask your doctor before you start playing racquetball; although fairly safe, it can be strenuous.

Racquetballs are all the same size and must meet the same specifications to be an official ball. Racquetballs are sold not only in cans, but also in boxes and bags. Racquetballs are made by pressing the two rubber sides together in a factory. The air inside the ball is not pressurized, nor is the can. Each ball has the same pressure, so the balls bounce consistently. However, because the outside air pressure is lower at higher altitudes, a ball in Denver, a mile (1.6 km) above sea level, is different than one in Winnipeg, Canada, which is below sea level. Some stores sell ball pressurizers. These yellow cans increase air pressure within the ball, but are only helpful for racquetball players trying to prepare for faster court conditions or higher-altitude play. Balls come in different colors, but all bounce the same for the reasons already mentioned.

Many players use a racquetball glove to keep the racket from slipping through their hands, but this is a personal choice. Gloves come in different materials, and some allow you to better feel the racket. I suggest keeping two or three gloves and changing them often during a match so that they do not get soaked. Once wet, the gloves do not last as long and may lose their elasticity.

Perhaps the most important piece of equipment is a pair of eye guards. During play, a racquetball moves quickly and could cause serious injury if it were to hit an unprotected eye. Think of a carpenter sawing wood as a helpful analogy to justify the use of eye guards: He wears protective eyewear not because he has ever gotten a splinter in his eye, but because it could happen. Racquetball

2 **Racquetball equipment.**

players should wear eyewear as a precautionary measure. See figure 2 for an example of an acceptable pair of eye guards, glove, ball, and racket.

Racquetball shoes are much like tennis shoes except that the soles are thinner because racquetball does not demand the jumping that tennis does. Here's a tip from veteran players: Use tennis shoes for practice because they will protect your feet, and use racquetball shoes for tournaments because they are lighter. This yields a psychological (and perhaps physical) advantage. When you wear your racquetball shoes, your feet will feel lighter, allowing faster movement in competitive matches.

A game of racquetball is played to a score of 15. The rally begins with the serve and ends with a winning shot. Like in volleyball, the person serving can score, and the person receiving the serve can only regain the serve. The receiver will not score a point for winning a rally, but will regain the serve. This affects strategy because it is more advantageous to take chances when serving, not when receiving the serve. Unforced errors while receiving the serve cost the player points. The object of the game is to get the ball back to the front wall before it bounces on the floor twice. Once the ball hits the floor twice, the rally is over. The ball may hit a wall after or before hitting the floor and still be in play because it has not bounced twice on the floor. This creates exciting play and random-movement conditioning.

Games are played to 15, and if there is a split, the third game is a tiebreaker to 11. There is no "win by two" or serving one side and then the other as in other racket or paddle sports. For a more detailed rulebook, write USA Racquetball (USAR) at 1685 W. Uintah, Colorado Springs, Colorado, 80904 or go to www.usaracquetball.com. You can download this rulebook free of charge. The USAR is the official governing body of racquetball. I strongly suggest joining if you play racquetball. Most tennis and golf aficionados reap benefits from belonging to their national organizations. The same is true of racquetball. You will be more supportive of our national governing body and receive great news and instructional information from the best players and coaches in the world.

The final thing new players should be aware of is etiquette. Here are a few rules to remember:

1. Always knock on the door before opening it. If someone is running to get a ball on an enclosed court and someone else opens the door, the results could be catastrophic.

2. Call "hinder" if someone is getting too close to you. A hinder occurs when player A is too close to player B, and player B cannot make her shot. Player B would have to stop play. A regular hinder results in a replay. An avoidable hinder results in loss of the rally. Avoidable hinders are those that could have been avoided and are sometimes controversial calls in tournament play. I advise recreational players to replay contested points. It is safer to call too many hinders than not enough. Often new players focus so much on the ball that they do not see the person in front of them and can injure them by swinging when they should hold up their swing.

3. Call against yourself. Remember to practice good sportsmanship. If a shot is not good, call it.

4. Have fun! It's okay to yell, laugh, cry, and vent emotions in this game. Racquetball is not like some of our cousin racket sports that take themselves so seriously. (However, refrain from yelling or talking during a rally. Talk that distracts your opponent is considered an avoidable hinder and is against the rules.)

5. Keep score audibly. Call out the score after every rally so that nobody loses track. Believe it or not, advanced players are often guilty of this, and even in the Pan American Games one year the referee lost track of the score. So call out the score.

In the coming chapters you will find information that will lead to successful racquetball workouts. You will find useful drills that enhance each chapter's lessons. Because racquetball is played with a partner (or partners, if you play doubles), I have included partner drills as well as solo drills. Each chapter includes tips and a few tricks of the trade. This information is geared toward beginners and progresses toward advanced-level players. I never have agreed with that axiom that *practice makes perfect*. I believe that *perfect practice makes perfect*. Thus, in the coming chapters the advanced practice tips supplement the basic fundamentals. You will not be able to put all this information into play immediately, but use the basic information now. Then come back to this book and use it as a reference for years of racquetball excellence.

Welcome to *Racquetball Fundamentals*.

Key to Diagrams

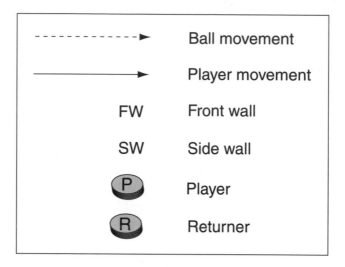

- - - - - - - -▶	Ball movement
───────▶	Player movement
FW	Front wall
SW	Side wall
P	Player
R	Returner

Serve

Play begins with the serve. The serve is the most important shot in the game because it dictates the return. A good serve may not end in an outright point, but it should bring about a desired return. For example, a player may want to overpower his opponent with low hard serves. Another option is to lull an aggressive player with slow high serves. Because the serve is the only shot that does not have to be hurried, a player should take his time executing it. Two types of serves are offensive and defensive. An offensive serve is like a fastball thrown by a baseball pitcher because the objective of this serve is to overpower your opponent. A defensive serve is similar to a change-of-speed pitch. It is designed to elicit a defensive return by throwing off an opponent's timing, causing him to lean too far forward in attacking the serve.

Drive Serve

The main offensive serve is the drive serve. The drive serve is a low hard serve designed as an offensive weapon. The object is to hit it low and hard into the opponent's backhand or forehand corner of the court. To hit a drive serve, draw an imaginary line from your waist to the front wall. Where this line meets the front wall is the *waist line*. Hit this imaginary spot, and the ball will rebound into the corner to the right-hander's left and left-hander's right. The *hand line* is formed by placing the racket hand straight out to the side and drawing an imaginary line from the end of the racket hand to the front wall. That imaginary point where this line meets the front wall is the hand line. The waist line is waist high on the front wall, and the hand line should be at the same height. When hitting the hand line, the ball will travel to the right-hander's right side of the court and the left-hander's left side of the court.

The imaginary line and subsequent spot on the front wall are easy to visualize and provide a target for the server. Looking at this imaginary line, the server begins to realize that the point on the front wall is almost in front of the server. This keeps the serve headed toward the corner and gives the server more room to relocate to center court after the serve. A tip for advanced racquetball: The lower the server can get, the harder it will be to return the serve because the serve also will be low.

Left-handers reverse this process; instead of aiming for the waist line, they aim for the hand line to go to the left. Aiming for the line from the waist will allow the left-hander to serve to the right. The left-handed player will want to serve most serves to the left corner when playing right-handed players.

If the server wants the ball to go into the left corner, she should aim at the spot where the hand line intersects the front wall. The ball will rebound into the right corner if this spot is hit. Look at the front wall and note where the hand line and the waist line reach the front wall. Note that these two spots are about a body's width apart. If the server hits in the middle of these two target areas, the ball will rebound and hit the server. When the server moves to the right or left in the service zone, the waist and hand targets move also and are easy to visualize.

You can execute footwork two ways on the drive serve. The first is the simpler one-step motion, and the second is a two-step motion, which is discussed in More to Choose and Use. In the one-step approach, the server simply drops the ball in front and to the right. The server steps straight forward and strikes the ball, aiming at the waist or hand targets (figure 1.1). The trick is to keep the weight back and forcefully release the hips, then use the body to drag the racket through the hitting zone. Because a loose arm provides more snap, let the arm go limp like spaghetti. Or to put it another way, you can hit the ball harder with a whip than you can with a board.

Upon striking the ball, the server must get out of the service zone and into center-court position as quickly as possible. Make sure the racket face is slightly open so that the ball will pass the second red line. (*Open* means the racket face points toward the ceiling. *Closed* means the face points toward the floor.) This is

1.1 **One-step serve.**

the short line, and any ball just over that line on the serve is a good serve. These aiming points will put the ball into the corners making it very difficult for the receiver to return the ball. The more open the racket face, the higher the ball will go to the opponent's backhand.

Two-Step Serve   The two-step approach on the drive serve is the same as the one step, except for the addition of a ministep to get started. This little step increases hip turn and allows the server to hit the ball harder, and if executed correctly, lower. The server takes a short first step (figure 1.2a) and a big second step (figure 1.2b). Notice that the toe points to the right corner. This takes pressure off the left knee and prevents injuries. Also notice how far away the server has to drop the ball. This is necessary to get the power and control needed. To provide the server enough time to get to the ball, the drop must be higher than on the one-step approach.

A good drive serve is not hit by leaning into the ball. This puts too much weight forward and makes it harder to relocate. Try not to hit the side wall. This will cause the ball to rebound into center court. For an advanced drive serve, strike the ball about shin high, an arm and a racket's length away, and follow through to knee height. This should put the ball just over the short line, headed toward the left back corner.

Two-Step Serve

1.2a   **Short first step.**

1.2b   **Big second step.**

To add variation, strike the drive serve two different ways. Strike from low to high, and then strike from high to low. For a low-to-high serve, hit the ball about shin high, and follow through to the knee so that the serve will stay low after it crosses the short line. The reverse, high to low, simply means that the server strikes the ball higher and aims the serve downward. A good rule is to strike the ball thigh high in the hitting zone and drive it down so that it goes over the short line. This causes a higher bounce on the floor for the receiver. Hitting low to high and high to low varies the serves and causes weak returns. Be sure to make use of the entire service zone when serving. Move a little to the right of center and then back toward the left wall. This creates serves of different angles. When varying the pace, going from the soft drive serve to the hard drive serve, an opponent's timing will be off for sure!

Lob Serve   The main defensive serve is the lob serve, designed to elicit a defensive return. It is a safe serve and is hard to fault. It is hit softly, so the receiver must provide most of the power for the return. The differences between the lob and the drive serve are simply trajectory and speed. The drive serve is a power serve, and the server provides the power. The lob serve is a finesse serve, and thus the power must be provided by the receiver. One of the primary benefits of the lob serve is that the server can reach center court quickly and be more balanced. Another benefit of the lob is that it should elicit a defensive or safe return, as opposed to the offensive serve, which is designed to win a point by forcing a weak return.

The lob can be struck several ways. For a good lob, open the racket face so that it points toward the ceiling. Think of cooking pancakes on a frying pan. Now, pull the racket in a backswing, and use your legs to push the ball upward on the front wall. This causes the ball to move in an upward trajectory. Aim for a spot about 12 to 14 feet (3.6–4.3 meters) high where the imaginary waist line meets the front wall. The ball will softly rebound into the back left corner. This puts more air under the ball and creates a softer serve. To increase accuracy, keep your head down, and try to keep your eyes on the ball even as it hits the racket on the serve (figure 1.3).

1.3   Lob serve.

5

The traditional lob serve is struck waist high and lifted softly into the back left or right corner. Because most players are right-handed, the lob left corner is a basic bread-and-butter serve. The left-hander must aim for the hand line to execute the same serve. Left-handed players should aim for a spot 12 to 14 feet (3.6–4.3 meters) high at the imaginary hand line spot on the front wall. They will discover a nice lob serve that moves toward the left wall.

Another trick is to hit lobs at different trajectories. In figure 1.4 the player is hitting a lob from a low bounce to a high spot on the front wall. The serve can be struck lower than normal, and the follow-through will be high like in a chest-high lob. A high-to-low serve would be struck approximately knee high and lifted to the front wall so that it hits about 16 feet (5 meters) high on the wall. The high-to-low serve is sometimes called the *Texas lob*, after its state of origin. This creates a pop-fly trajectory; when the ball bounces in the receiving area, it bounces very high. This high bounce forces a player to hit the ball above her head, thus losing control of the return. The high-to-low serve is usually struck in an overhand manner. The server strikes the ball above her head like a tennis serve (remember, you must let the ball bounce high off the floor because you cannot hit a ball out of the air like in tennis). The point on the wall is about 8 to 10 feet (2.4–3 meters) high, and the ball will travel in a more downward manner over the short line. It is still a soft serve, but with a different trajectory.

Spin can help a good lob serve. Be sure to follow through over the ball when hitting the lob. This puts topspin on the serve and causes a high bounce into the backcourt (figure 1.5). Another trick is to use underspin. Imagine that the ball is the face of a clock. If you strike the ball at four o'clock and follow through over the ball, you have used topspin. If you strike the ball at five o'clock and follow through under the ball, you have used underspin. Both types of spin

1.4 **Low-to-high lob serve.**

put the ball deep into center court. Another tip on the lob serve is to aim very high on the back left wall so that the ball drops almost straight down into the left corner. This serve is called the *lob nick* because it nicks the left wall high and drops down, pinning the receiver into the back left corner.

Soft Drive Serve A hybrid of the hard drive serve and the lob serve is the soft drive serve. This is still an offensive serve, but it takes less energy to hit. It also confuses the opponent because it looks like it is going to be a hard serve, but is a soft serve. This causes the receiver to put too much weight forward and throws her timing off. When describing this serve, racquetball players often say the receiver was too far out in front, which means that the receiver had too much weight forward.

Think of the soft drive serve as a low lob serve. Instead of hitting the ball at 100 percent effort, hit at 60 percent. This throws off an opponent's timing and helps you remain balanced and prepared to play the serve return. The soft drive server is hit the same as a drive serve except that the server hits the serve and moves back almost in one motion. This puts the server into center-court position faster. The combination of an off-speed serve and the server moving back confuses the receiver and allows the server easy shots in the frontcourt.

1.5 Topspin follow through.

Take it to the court

Game Tempo

The game tempo is the timing of play. Players can rush serves and play, or they may vary the tempo and play slowly and deliberately, using soft serves. A good analogy is the fast break in basketball, which is like the power game and favors the talented speedy athlete.

The slow deliberate style of basketball and racquetball may put the talented athlete at a disadvantage if he is not patient.

When hitting serves be aware of game control. The game of racquetball is one of tempo, and the very best players control the tempo. Often, with adrenaline running through their veins, players lose sight of this. The object of the game is not so much playing at the tempo you like, but at the tempo your opponent dislikes. As a general rule, players who love to hit the ball hard are called power players. Power players hate lobs. Players who have great technique and control are called control players. Control players hate the power game. Within this framework it is possible to make both drive and lob serves more effective. The player has 10 seconds to put the ball into play after the score is called in a tournament. No rule says you cannot put the ball into play almost immediately after the score is called. This makes the drive-serve game or power game more effective. You can also wait the full 10 seconds to hit the lob serve. This makes the lob-serve game or control game more effective.

Another subtle lob tip is to adjust your body posture. Imagine yourself as a confident, maybe even cocky, athlete. Take that posture and wait. Racquetball veterans call it the *swagger*. This sends a message to your opponent and may even irritate her a tad. This swagger and waiting 10 seconds to begin your lob serve often add to the suspense the receiver feels when all she wants to do is play, but has to wait for you to begin play. One way to have swagger is to put all your weight on your right hip. Pull your shoulders up straight, put your head back, and look bored. That is swagger!

In a drive serve, think of yourself as a blitzing defense in football. A blitzing defense attacks. The quarterback has no time to throw the ball because the other players are swarming all over him. That swarm is a blitzing defense. When attacking an opponent with a drive serve try to maintain that blitzing mentality. Try to hurry the rallies and swarm over your opponent. (The rally begins with the serve and ends with a winning shot.) This makes you more aggressive in shot selection and makes your opponent vulnerable when you change tempos from slow sleepy lobs to fast-paced action.

It is up to the athlete to recognize the importance of the rhythm and control the tempo of the game. One way to practice varying your tempo is to use the famous strategy of Bill Walsh, the San Francisco 49ers football coach. He used to script the first 20 plays for his team. You can do the same with serves. This reminds novice player to vary their tempo. Script 10 different lob and drive serves to begin a match. As a rule of thumb, when in doubt over what tempo to play, think of the most successful tempo you have employed. See chapter 9 for more details on controlling the tempo and pace of the game.

Game situations often dictate tempo. When ahead and close to the end of a game, speed it up and finish him off. This dictates a faster paced game at the end, especially if it has been slower throughout the game. Try to save a special serve for the end. Many games are won by different serves or variations. Remember, all you have to do is get your opponent to shoot from the backcourt so you can cover the front. He may hit a perfect shot, but odds are an unforced error or a shot left up in the frontcourt will play to your advantage. Remember this: The floor beats most people, and if you can help your opponent lose to the floor, then so be it.

Give it a go

SERVE DRILL

Those who play racquetball's cousin sport tennis have practiced serves for years. A tennis player will take a bucket of balls to the court to practice serves. Racquetball players should do the same. Take a small plastic bucket of balls to the court and hit drive serves in sets of 10. Chart the good serves. What is a good serve? A good serve crosses the short line and bounces twice on the floor before hitting the back wall. A good drive serve drops into the area in the backcourt you were aiming for, usually the back left or right corners. Chart the percentages so you can strive for improvement each time you perform this drill (table 1.1). The same drill can be done with lob serves, with the same objective to improve percentages of good serves.

Table 1.1

PERCENTAGE OF GOOD SERVES				
Skill	10	10	10	%
Drive serve	8	4	3	50%
Lob serve	4	3	6	43%

AIR DRILL

Beginning players often have trouble with hand–eye coordination. Take a racket and bounce the ball on the strings as long as possible, getting the feel of the ball on the strings. When you become proficient at this, reverse the racket side when the ball is in midair. Each time the ball bounces up off the strings, turn your hand and racket over, either palm up or palm down, and bounce the ball. This creates a forehand-backhand air drill.

TAP DRILL

For racket control, stand about five to six feet (1.5–2 meters) away from the side wall and tap the ball into the wall repeatedly using a forehand grip and a controlled tap. Try this drill backhanded. For an advanced tap drill, switch every tap from forehand to backhand. This is an excellent way to gain control, because the drill is impossible without proper body balance and racket technique (figure 1.6).

1.6   **Tap drill.**

FIVE-POINT DRIVE-SERVE GAME

With a partner, play the five-point drive-serve-only game. The object of this game is to improve your serve. In the drive-serve game the player can use only the drive serve (figure 1.7). The server and receiver can score on each rally. This is called *rally scoring* and, of course, differs from regular rules where only the server scores. One player serves every serve, win or lose, in a five-point game. Use rally scoring, and the first serving player to get to five wins.

Because the server only hits drive serves, the players work exclusively on serving and returning these serves. The players should agree on which side to serve to so that they only work on one side. The rules can be changed based on the sides the players want to work on. If player A wants to work on drive serves to the right, the drilling partner, player B, will receive the serve and work on offensive returns. This allows player A not only to work on the serve, but also on the rekills off that serve. After five points the players switch, and player B works on the same side.

This drill can also be done with the lob serve. This time player A works on lobs to the right. Player B receives the serve on the right side. Player A tries to hit good lobs, and player B works on offensive or defensive returns. If player A hits a poor lob, player B hits an offensive return, and if player A hits a good lob, player B must hit a defensive return.

1.7   **Five-point drive-serve game.**

FIVE-POINT SERVE GAME

The five-point serve game can also be played like a regular game. The players still use rally scoring like a regular game of racquetball, but the players must score five points in a row. If they score only four points, it is a side out. A winning game is five points scored in a row. This is not easy to achieve when the game is played between two equally matched players. Because this practice game simulates what a real game might look like, players use all their serves and vary their tempo, thus working on game control.

Forehand

The forehand stroke is executed from the right side of the court if the player is right-handed and the left side of the court if left-handed. Hitting a forehand uses the same skill as hitting a serve. Because most serves are struck with the forehand stroke, practicing the serve is essential to improving the forehand skills. The basic forehand stroke has been likened to skipping a rock or throwing sidearm. All use the same motion. Another way of thinking about the forehand is to imagine a tennis serve. The arm extends up and over the head to strike the ball in a motion called *overhand*. Take that same motion, but move it to the side of the athlete, and that is a racquetball forehand stroke.

Establishing Grip and Mechanics

2.1   The proper grip.

The proper forehand mechanics are much like throwing sidearm, skipping a rock, or batting. The stroke begins with the proper grip. To use the proper grip, shake hands with the racket. Your thumb and forefinger should form a V as pictured in figure 2.1. A grip at the one o'clock to two o'clock position on the racket allows a player to hit the ball at full extension. The closer the player grips the racket toward the two o'clock area, the flatter the stroke will be. The player should squeeze with the top two fingers and guide with the bottom three. This is called the trigger-finger grip. This grip is crucial because it is the only grip that allows the player to hit the ball out and away.

If a player grips the racket with an O grip (no V between the thumb and forefinger), she must strike the ball by twisting her wrist and hitting the ball when it is too close to her body. This twist-stroke imperfection makes execution more difficult. Not only does this imperfection hurt a player's consistency, it hurts a player's body. The wrong grip causes a player to use a downward stroke, or a pendulum swing, which causes overuse injuries by putting stress on the lower back, shoulder, wrist, and elbow.

Once you are gripping your racket correctly, you can prepare to hit the ball. Three steps comprise the proper ready position. They are a ready racket, feet toward the side wall, and a balanced stance. The first step is the racket readiness or *racket prep.* This simply means you should carry the racket comfortably above your waist. Dropping the racket below your waist lengthens your swing. Rather than just a forehand swing, you will need a swing and a half to bring the racket into ready position. Carrying the racket above your waist leads to a faster preparation with less room for error. As soon as you know the shot is coming to your forehand side, the racket should be up and ready to hit. You must raise your hitting elbow to a little lower than shoulder height. Your racket should be in a *salute* position (figure 2.2a). This is similar to a military salute, except that the racket is out and away from your head rather than close to it like the saluting hand would be. This position takes pressure off your shoulder. Holding your racket too close to your head can also cause a longer swing or excess motion.

Another key to an effective forehand is to get the feet to the side wall. Notice that in figure 2.2a, the player's feet are at the side wall, which allows the player to hit with more power and balance. It is natural to face the front wall and shoot the ball. However, this limits shot selection because the player will have to hit crosscourt. This poor form will also lead to overuse injuries because it stresses the arm and shoulder. The third key to a good stroke is a balanced stance. When positioning the feet to the side wall, you should have the feet a little wider than shoulder-width apart. The weight should be on the balls of the feet and balanced. The hips should be low. This athletic position will enable you to hit with maximum power and control.

The forehand uses out-and-around stroke mechanics, and the progression is from the shoulder to the elbow, wrist, and then racket. Thus the stroke has a flat trajectory, leaving less room for error, but more important, less stress on the shoulder and elbow. One saying you can remember to improve your game is "the more shoulder, elbow, wrist, racket, the harder you whack it." The player begins with her rear hip and hitting elbow driving forward, almost as if they were connected. Figure 2.2b shows the impact point in the hitting zone and figure 2.2c shows the follow-through. Notice how level the athlete's shoulders are and how low the follow-through is. Also notice the wrist rollover on the follow-through. This allows for topspin that keeps the ball down after it hits the front wall.

2.2a Setup. | **2.2b** Impact point. | **2.2c** Follow-through.

2.3 The power zone.

2.4 Low forearm angle for forehand.

Where to Strike the Ball

Players should strive to hit the ball when it is aligned with the midline area of their bodies. This area is known as the *power zone.* The power zone is that area from the inner thigh of the back leg to the front leg. Any ball struck within this zone will be hit with maximum power. The best way to illustrate the power zone is to lay three rackets on the floor (figure 2.3). The first racket is behind the power zone, and any ball struck there will hit the side wall. The second racket is in the power zone, and any ball hit there will go straight in and come straight back. The third racket is in front of the power zone, and balls will go crosscourt when struck there. The power zone is also an arm and a racket's length away from the body.

Stroke Mechanics Improving forearm angle and wrist flexion will improve the mechanics of the forehand. The higher the forearm above the elbow, the lower the player can hit the ball. When the forearm drops below the elbow, the ball will rise up on the front wall (figure 2.4). Using the wrist also helps mechanics. Snap the wrist forward at the end of the stroke to generate racket-head speed. To accomplish this, imagine the handle of the racket pointed toward the front wall. This should happen just before racket extension. This last part of the forehand is the snap of the whip that produces power.

Using the information in the previous section about the power zone, you can develop adjustment strategies during a game to determine why the ball went where it did. When the ball hits the side wall, it must have been struck behind the power zone. If the ball goes down the wall straight, it must have been struck in the power zone. Any ball traveling crosscourt must have been struck in front of the power zone.

You can adjust to balls struck too high on the front wall also. If the ball goes up, the player tilted the shoulders up, and conversely, if the ball goes down, the shoulders were tilted down. Technically, the face of the racket was facing up if the ball went up, and was facing down if the ball went down. However, it is very difficult to control the face of the racket and very easy to control the shoulders. All an athlete has to do is adjust his shoulders or his hitting area in the power zone if the ball is not going where he wants it to go (figure 2.5a-b). Of course, this feedback system can also be used for the serve. If the drive serve goes short, the athlete must simply tilt his shoulders up a little more.

Forehand Shot

| 2.5a | Setting up the forehand. | 2.5b | Adjusting shoulders in power zone. |

Proximity to the Ball   Keep the ball away from you. This will give your forehand greater force and more options. Notice that if a player is too close to the ball, it limits his shot options and he must hit the side wall or go crosscourt. If the player stays away from the ball, he can hit any shot he wants because he is far enough away from the ball. He will have the leverage to go down the line or crosscourt. Also, remember that the power zone is one arm's length and one racket away from the body. If the player hits the ball too close to his body he must twist his wrist, which causes him to lose the force of the swing. This limits his options.

Take it to the court

Balance

To create balance, remember two things. First, keep the knees under the hips. This sounds rather straightforward. How can the knees not be under the hips? If the athlete takes a big step, he will overstep his stance and lose power. More important, he will have to drag one leg instead of being able to push with each leg. The other forehand balance cue is to keep the weight on the balls of the feet. In figure 2.6 we see a player leaning forward. This is a natural thing to do, but balance, control, and power are lost because the athlete has all his weight forward. Because the athlete is off balance, he will have to take a false step to make another step. For balance and control, keep more weight back (figure 2.7).

2.6   Incorrect, off-balance stance.

2.7   Correct stance.

DROP-AND-HIT DRILL

The drop-and-hit drill is great. Drop and hit forehands in all of the three zones: forward, behind, and the power zone. If the ball is in front, work on crosscourt shots. If the ball is behind, work on pinch shots, which hit the side wall. If the ball is in the power zone, hit the ball down the line. Work on the fundamentals of keeping your weight back, pointing the handle toward the front wall before impact, and hitting out and around, not up and down. Be sure to stay an arm and a racket's length away from the ball.

SETUP-AND-HIT DRILL

The setup-and-hit drill is next. Gently tap the ball to the front wall, and after the ball bounces once on the floor, hit the ball in the power zone for a down-the-line shot. The ball should bounce around the service line off the front wall, so the striking should be to the right of center court at the receiving line (dotted line) or slightly behind it. If the setup is not good and is too high, hit a ceiling ball or defensive shot for good shot selection practice.

A variation of the same setup drill is the multiple-offense drill. A setup is an easy scoring opportunity. Tap setups to yourself by hitting soft one-bounce shots off the front wall and work on hitting forehands in front of the power zone (crosscourt shots), down-the-line shots (in the power zone), and behind-the-power-zone pinch shots (shots that hit the side wall).

RACKET-DOWN-THE-SHIRT DRILL

Use the racket-down-the-shirt trick to keep from bending at the waist when hitting a forehand. (Of course, this works with forehand mechanics, too.) Take a racket and put it down your shirt with the face of the racket against your chest. Stuff the handle into the waistband of your shorts, and hit a few forehands at half speed. This keeps you from bending at the waist and helps remind you to bend at the knees and not the waist.

FOREHAND GAME

Play a full game with a partner, but change the rules to favor the forehand practice. The player who wins a point with her forehand gets two points. A player who wins a point with a backhand gets one point. This will put more emphasis on the forehand stroke.

FOREHAND HUMAN BALL MACHINE

Find a partner to play as a human ball machine, which will help with hitting forehands. The practice partner simply hits 10 setups to the player. Keep track of the percentages of perfect kill shots off setups, and the highest percentage wins. A kill shot is defined many ways, but is essentially an unreturnable shot. This competition keeps a player focused on improving forehand skills.

FIVE-POINT GAMES

The five-point games mentioned in chapter 1 for serve skills also develop forehand skills if the serve is focused on the forehand side of the court.

Court Positioning

Good court positioning and positioning between shots can make a slow player much faster, and poor court positioning can make a fast player very slow. It is not necessarily the faster person who wins, but the person in the best position. To find where that good position is between rallies, we must first examine the court. The halfway line of the court is the short line. It is there that we find ourselves exactly 20 feet (6 meters) from the front wall.

If the ball strikes the front wall at a point six inches (15 cm) or less off the floor, it will bounce the second time within a foot (30 cm) of the short line. Therefore, if a player's psychological approach is, "I'm going to get every ball no matter how low you hit it," he will only be able to lift up these shots as he scoops them off the floor. The player who is behind them will step up, hit the shot, and leave the retriever out of position. If a player is too close to the front wall, she opens up the passing lanes. It is much easier to execute a passing shot than a kill shot. Therefore, the first rule of defense is to prevent the pass by positioning yourself deep, playing behind the receiving line (the dotted line). This forces the opponent to hit a kill shot, a much more difficult shot to hit.

Positioning Yourself

3.1 Correct court position for a right-hander's center court relocation.

After the serve, relocate to the center of the court just behind the dotted receiving lines. This puts you in the best position to retrieve as many shots as possible. If you step over to the left toward the side wall, you will find yourself able to cover the entire left side. If the crossover step is to the right, the opposite is true.

When moving to the left, keep the ball in sight. Never take your eyes off the ball—here is where those eye guards come in handy. Without the eye guards, it would be a tricky process to watch the ball safely. Keep your feet positioned diagonal to the front wall. The right-handed player's left foot should be slightly staggered back from his right foot (figure 3.1), and the left-handed player's right foot should be staggered apart from the left (figure 3.2). This will put the relocated server in position to see the ball without having to shift his weight. If the server faces the front wall, he cannot see the ball behind him and will have to react to the ball rebounding off the front wall. This cuts down the time available to get to the next shot, plus it leaves the defensive player vulnerable to a pinch shot. If the receiver hits a side wall, the defensive player will move in the same direction that she first sees the ball. If she is waiting for it to come into her field of vision from the front wall, she will move the wrong way.

3.2 Correct court position for a left-hander's center court relocation.

Almost as bad as facing the front wall is pointing the feet toward the side wall. This player facing the side wall is in great position if his opponent hits a shot down that wall. However, if the player goes crosscourt, the side-wall facing player must make two steps to go nowhere just to get back to a balanced position, a position he should have been in from the start. The solution to these problems of facing the front or side wall is to imagine a diagonal line from the left back corner to right front corner and another line from the right back corner to left front corner (figure 3.3). When the ball is on the left side of the court, proper positioning is along that line from left back to right front. When the ball is on the right side of the court, proper positioning is on the line from left front to right back.

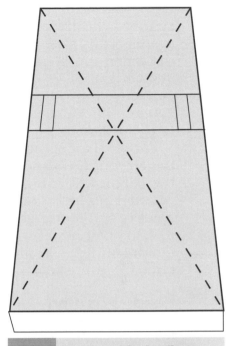

3.3   **Court positioning lines.**

Be sure to move your weight back during the serve. This move takes practice, but as mentioned in chapter 1, it is important to keep your weight back. This not only allows a better serve, but it also allows a better push into center court. By keeping your weight back and pushing back with the back leg, you can get to center court faster (figure 3.4). If you put too much weight on the front foot, you will go off to the side and will lose a step getting to center court. Keeping the weight back, hitting a drive serve, and moving back at the same time can be a little tricky because the serve must be hit before making any movement back toward center court. It is very difficult to hit the serve and move back at the same time. Therefore, think of it this way: Instead of using 100 percent effort to hit the serve, use 80 percent, and save 20 percent to move into center-court position.

3.4   **Pushing to center court.**

Moving to the Ball   Stay balanced and positioned along the imaginary diagonal line from corner to corner. This allows you to move to the next shot. Stay balanced by keeping your knees comfortably spaced beneath your hips. This may sound elementary, but if you overstep this axis, you will end up with your weight over one leg or the other and be unable to push with both legs to get to the next shot. If you overstep and stretch to a ball and don't hit the shot perfectly, you will have a difficult time getting to the next shot. If you do not overstep to the ball, you can push with both feet to get to the next shot.

Rather than sprinting to center court, flow to this magical position. If you run full speed to center court and your opponent mis-hits the ball, it will waft gently past you as you sprint into center-court position. Therefore, move to center court; don't run. Take on the identity of a soccer goalie who will not let a ball get by, as opposed to a football player who sprints toward the goal line. This flowing movement helps keep you under control and able to change directions to get to shots.

Ready Position   Before each shot during the rally, come to ready position. In ready position your knees are slightly bent, your butt is low, and you are ready to move toward any shot. Remember to keep your racket above the waist. This is very important because often the ball arrives before a player is ready. The reflex shot, or volley as it is called in tennis, is executed best when the racket is above the waist. If the racket is below the waist, the ball will be lifted. Baseball players, volleyball players, and athletes in most sports have to be ready by being in athletic or ready position. In racquetball the trick is to be ready for each shot. Because of the random-movement nature of this game it is not always possible, but striving for perfection will allow you to get to more shots and play much better defense. Anticipate your opponent's shot using the following cues, but do not simply guess at your opponent's shot. A guess is 66 percent wrong, but an anticipated move is 66 percent correct!

Read Your Opponent's Shot   Pay close attention to your opponent so that you can anticipate the next move she'll make, and you will be prepared for the next shot. Here are key physical signs to watch for from your opponent:

1. Watch your opponent's shoulders. If your opponent dips his shoulder, he is going to shoot low, and you may be able to cheat up a little in positioning, or move forward on the court. You should be ready to hit an offensive shot. If the shoulders tilt up,

the shot probably will be a defensive shot. Sag a little deeper in the center-court zone to play the ball in the backcourt.

2. Watch your opponent's hips. If the player opens up, or faces forward with her hips, she is probably going crosscourt. Therefore cheat a little toward the crosscourt side. If the hips stay closed, she is going down the line. Play closer to the immediate side to prevent a down-the-line pass.

3. Watch your opponent's feet. If he steps toward the side wall, he is probably going to hit the side wall, and the ball will hit in the center of the frontcourt after hitting the side wall. If you detect this, move up to cover the shot.

4. Sense your opponent. This is difficult to teach, but after playing someone for a long time, you can sense where she will go with the ball. The excellent players learn where their opponents will hit the ball in a short time by sensing.

Dictate Your Opponent's Shots   If the ball is on the left side of the court, cheat slightly to the left because it takes longer for the ball to go crosscourt, and you can catch up with it. In figure 3.5, the player has hit a serve into the left corner, and the receiver of the serve is pinned in the left corner. Notice the position of the server. He has positioned himself behind the dotted line and slightly to the left of center. The receiver has the entire front wall to aim toward, and the server is not in her way. Note that if the server took one more step left he would be blocking shots crosscourt, and if he moved one step over to the right, he would be way out of position. When the opponent goes crosscourt, the server has far more time to get to the ball.

3.5   **Cheating to the left.**

If the ball goes down the line, it is harder to retrieve, so cheating left makes it easier to retrieve down the lines and provides time to cover the crosscourt shots.

Stay behind the dotted line. This line is called the receiving line. A player is not allowed to hit the ball before it strikes the floor in this area. A player in front of the line is too close to the front wall. As mentioned before, staying behind the line puts the player in the best position to retrieve shots and provides the best angles for covering crosscourt and down-the-line shots.

As you become more comfortable it becomes important to learn stunting. Every football player knows that *stunting* is the term used when the defensive linemen shift into another defense at the snap, thereby "stunting" the offense. In racquetball you can do the same thing. Play deep in the zone of center court, and move up upon impact, gambling that your opponent will attempt a pinch shot or low shot up front. Of course, you can do the opposite. Play up deep and move back quickly, anticipating a passing shot. A word of warning here: This is a gambling defense and there is a 33 percent chance that you will guess wrong. But a few good guesses puts a ton of pressure on an offensive player.

Know Your Opponent   By doing homework, you can eliminate a lot of guesswork from a match. Years ago I was asked to coach an up-and-coming player on the men's professional racquetball tour. He gave me a videotape of a top Canadian athlete he had defeated in the first round. Because it was a first-round match played on a Wednesday afternoon, few people were in the stands. One person stood out from the crowd. His name was Drew Kachtik, from Texas, the number one player in the world at that time. I did not know exactly why Drew was watching this match, but I had a good idea. Sure enough, the next match this kid played was against Drew Kachtik. Drew was scouting this young player. Drew did not make the same mistakes in strategy that the Canadian had, and Drew defeated the young player soundly. Watching the opponent that you'll be playing allows you to get an idea of what shots that player likes to hit and will improve your ability to anticipate.

Center- and Deep-Court Positioning

Try relocating into center court after hitting a shot. Put an X in the center of the court on the dotted line. Work to come back to that X during rallies. Make sure your feet are slightly diagonal and not facing the front or side walls. Work to relocate along the imaginary corner-to-corner diagonal line. If the ball is hit into the center, not only is it impossible, but it is illegal, to relocate there because you could block your opponent's attempt to return the ball to the front wall. Your best option in this case is to stay behind your opponent, and try not to give him shots in the center of the court.

When the ball is in deep court, your relocation needs change. If the ball is 36 to 38 feet (11–11.5 meters) deep and in the backcourt, a defensive shot may be needed. If your opponent hits a defensive shot, stay a body width and a half away in the backcourt (figure 3.6). This puts pressure on the opponent to hit a perfect shot chest high and in the deep court. The odds are against this unless the players are at a professional level, in which case the rules change. But for our purposes, the body-width-and-a-half rule works. The best way to practice these movements is to play more racquetball! The more you play, the more familiar you will become with relocation court positioning.

3.6 Body-width-and-a-half rule.

AIR POSITIONING DRILL

Hit an imaginary serve and move back as fast as possible into center court. Put masking tape on the court, marking where to step and where to drop the ball. Work to *push back* against the serve so you can get into center-court positioning.

STAR DRILL

The player moves to the left corner of the frontcourt and hits an imaginary shot, and then backpedals to center court. The player then moves to the front right corner and repeats the backpedal motion to center court. Then the player moves to the back right corner, to center, to the back left corner, and then to center. The four corners make an imaginary star, and thus the name of the drill. This drill will familiarize you with proper court movements.

HIT AND GET DRILL

Play a game of multibounce racquetball. Hit the ball back to the front wall, and move into center court after every shot. This can be done with an opponent or alone. A word of caution: This is very strenuous, so start slowly and work your way up to longer rallies.

READ THE OPPONENT DRILL

Have a drill partner go to the back left corner. She will toss a ball into the corner, hitting the back wall first. She will track the ball out of the corner and attempt a return to the front wall. Try to read the shot, then go to it and rekill it. This is an excellent drill for reading shoulders, hips, and steps to determine shot coverage.

FISH-IN-A-NET GAME

Play this game with an opponent who has slightly lower skills, and try to run him all over the court, keeping the ball in play. Running your opponent side to side and up and back creates the *fish in a net*. In other words, you are in control, and he is like the poor fish. Your practice partner will love this because he gets a great workout and gets to play a better player. By trying to make your opponent run, you will work on retrieving skills and defensive skills as well as racket skills. Of course, the number one skill you will work on is positioning. If you are not adept at positioning yourself, you cannot do well in this game.

ZONE DEFENSE DRILL

Using tape, make a circle in deep center court (figure 3.7). As the ball travels, operate within that zone and do not leave it except to retrieve shots. If the ball is in deep court, rotate to the deep part of the zone. If it is in the frontcourt, rotate to the front part of the zone. This practice aid will help improve your relocation skills.

3.7 **Zone defense drill.**

Backhand

The backhand stroke should help a player cover half of the court. The right-handed player must use the backhand on the left side, and the left-hander on the right side. A beginning player tends to use the forehand for three-quarters of the court. While that strategy may work for a while, as the player becomes better she will discover that the advanced player exploits that type of shot selection.

The backhand is the exact opposite of the forehand. That message contains good news and bad news. The good news is that the backhand is not difficult to master. The bad news is that to do that, the player must do everything opposite from the forehand, and that is why the backhand carries the stigma of being difficult to learn. I believe that the United States sports culture is forehand friendly. Throwing is integral to many of our sports, and the forehand is a natural extension of that motion. The backhand requires the opposite movement, and many racquetball instructors explain the backhand by saying the stroke is different from the forehand. The mechanics are the same on both sides, but the motions are opposite. In fact, if you were to run a film of a forehand backward, you would see a perfect backhand stroke.

Traditional Backhand

4.1 Ready position.

4.2 Staggering the lead foot.

Use a backhand any time the ball is hit to the left of center, or if you are left-handed, when the ball is hit right of center. Before the ball even gets to the front wall, position the racket into ready position (figure 4.1). Take the racket and make a U with the racket as one side of the U, the forearm as the bottom, and the upper arm as the other side. Rest the U, or your arm and racket form, against your chest. Then, extend the U away from your body about six inches (15 cm) by moving the forearm away from your chest. Pull the arm back by pulling your hitting elbow six inches (15 cm) behind your hitting shoulder. Don't forget that early racket preparation will make the backhand more accurate.

Be prepared to track the ball with your feet toward the left wall if you are right-handed and toward the right wall if you are left-handed. Then you must reverse the forehand mechanics. Your lead foot should be staggered toe to instep (figure 4.2), which is the opposite foot movement of the forehand. In the forehand, a left-hander's right foot is slightly more toward the left side wall, and a right-hander's left foot is more toward the right side wall. When switching to the backhand it is normal to want to keep the feet the same; however, the right-hander's right leg is more toward the side wall, and the left-hander's left leg is more toward the side wall.

Start the stroke with the back of the body, not the front. The stroke begins by moving the left side of your body away from the ball and then toward the ball if you are right-handed. A left-handed player will turn her right side slightly away from the ball and then toward it. I like to call this the *turn-away-and-turn-in* move. Some instructors refer to this as *coil and uncoil.* Turn away when the ball hits the floor, and then turn into the ball. This is roughly the timing you should use to execute the backhand effectively.

The proper grip is the reverse grip of the forehand. The V formed by the thumb and forefinger should be at approximately 10 to 11 o'clock. Keep the racket out and around, not up and down, as is the tendency to do when learning the backhand. Hit out and away, imitating the motion of throwing a Frisbee. The racket makes contact with the ball in the power zone (figure 4.3). Reverse your footwork from the forehand stroke. A right-handed player hitting a backhand will step over with the right foot, not the left. A left-hander will step over with the left foot. The first movement in a backhand is a counter-rotation, so the player actually turns away prior to hitting the ball. The progression is the same as the forehand, shoulder, elbow, wrist, racket used in the forehand stroke. Notice that the hitting elbow is behind the front shoulder.

The follow-through should be level (figure 4.4). If the follow-through is high, the racket may have moved out of the power zone too early. An excellent way to think of the follow-through is to visualize 10 perfect hits in a row. Visualizing 10 balls in a row will help keep the racket level through the zone. Be sure to let the wrist roll naturally on the follow-through, as well. This adds topspin to the ball and helps keep it down. This wrist roll also puts less stress on the arm, because stopping the follow-through stresses the elbow and shoulder.

4.3 **Contact in the power zone.**

4.4 **Level follow-through.**

Traditional Backhand: Out and Around   The traditional backhand is hit in an out-and-around motion. The idea is to keep the racket face toward the front wall so that the plane of the swing is parallel to the floor throughout the swing. This means that the frame of the racket should face the floor with the strings facing the front wall through most of the power zone. The analogy of throwing a Frisbee is often used to explain the correct motion.

One way that backhand strokes evolve incorrectly is when the player swings up and down in a pendulum style. This may injure the lower back, shoulders, elbow, and even the wrist. Out-and-around mechanics alleviate stress in three parts of body. The first place stress is reduced is the elbow. Striking the ball over and over near the body increases stress on the elbow and causes tendinitis. The second place stress is reduced is in the shoulders. Striking the ball too close to the body puts stress on the hitting shoulder. The third place stress is reduced is in the lower back. A left-handed player reduces stress to his lower-right back, and a right-hander reduces stress to his lower-left back. The back stress occurs because the upper body is used more than the legs when striking the ball too close. This puts pressure on the lower back. Following the out-and-around method alleviates these problems.

New Backhand: Salute   This is the backhand of the new wave of players. This backhand is a simple salute to the ball (figure 4.5a), and, rather than out and around, it uses a shortened swing (figure 4.5b). The stroke is more compact because the torso is used. This shorter swing has the potential to make the shot more accurate. The salute backhand favors a shorter compact player with a strong abdomen and a strong lower back. The stronger and more compact a player's body, the more compact the swing can be. I suggest looking at your body type to figure out which stroke works best for you. Neither stroke is much different than the other because both address the ball away from the body, and both allow for maximum power and control.

Salute Backhand

4.5a Salute to the ball.

4.5b Shortened swing.

Take it to the court

Common Backhand Problems

Racket preparation can cause huge problems in forehand and backhand stroke mechanics. As soon as you see the ball traveling to the middle-court to left-wall area, your racket should be up, and your feet should start to move toward the left wall. Be sure to get your feet to the left wall as soon as possible and execute the crossover step with the right leg for right-handed players and with the left leg for left-handed players. Both feet should face the wall, and the lead hip should be *loaded*, or turned away from the front wall as you track the ball. The worst thing you can do is travel to the ball with your hip open (or facing the front wall) as you track the ball. This causes you to push the ball rather than to strike it, because the hips and legs are unable to generate power if the hips are facing the front wall. You will find most shots going crosscourt when the ball is struck in front of the stance.

Be careful not to develop a *spinning* backhand. Spinning into the ball occurs when the player sets both feet, but uses no hip motion. Instead, he provides power by spinning in his stance in a circular motion. Imagine the old bucket of water trick we did when we were kids, where the water inside a spinning bucket did not fall out. This trick illustrates centrifugal force. The centrifugal-force backhand technique ignores hip rotation and pushing forward with the back leg. To hit a correct backhand, shift your weight and hips slightly forward, and then rotate your hips into the ball. After you shift your weight forward, you will shift slightly back and hit with force from your back leg. An easier way to think about it is to put 60 percent of your weight on your back leg and 40 percent on your front leg. This will help establish balance and create power, because you will be able to use your hips and legs to push into the ball. If you put more weight forward, such as 80 percent, your back leg will be unable to provide power. This balance technique also allows for more control when striking the ball, because the athlete has her hips and legs under her and is balanced.

Avoid the impulse to run around the backhand by trying to hit a forehand; this makes it impossible to cover the court. Although matches at a lower level can be won by hitting a forehand from the left side of the court, at an advanced level of play the shot must be perfect. If it is not, the entire right side of the court will be left uncovered. The backhand cannot be mastered unless the left side of the court is used to hit a backhand.

Sometimes timing becomes an issue when a player performs a backhand shot. A great backhand technique is to turn away from the ball as the ball bounces on the floor. This provides momentum when hitting a backhand. A slight counterturn increases hitting control and power. Timing is important, but here's a good guideline: When the ball bounces on the floor, rotate slightly. Don't twist the body like a pretzel. Instead, turn away slightly, and then turn into the ball. See table 4.1 for other common backhand mistakes and solutions.

Table 4.1

Backhand Error Checklist

Symptom	Correction
No power	Don't open body too soon
Hitting side wall	Hit ball in power zone, not too far back in stance
Hitting crosscourt	Hit ball in power zone, not too far forward in stance; don't position hitting elbow in front of shoulder
Hitting too high	Keep front (right) shoulder down
Skipping (hitting too low)	Raise front shoulder slightly
Sore elbow on outside of arm	Hit out more, not down
Sore elbow at joint	Don't lock out backhand
Sore back	Don't bend at the waist

Give it a go

Cliff Swain has won more professional titles than any other player in the history of the game. His coach, former number one player in the world, Dave Peck, taught him some of the following drills as a junior player. Many of these movement and body control drills for the backhand are the same as for the forehand. Although many players do these drills, it is not the drills that make the player better, it is the perfect execution and attention to detail when performing these drills that make them better.

Some of the drills in other chapters also apply to improving the backhand technique. Follow the instructions in the "Give It a Go" sections in the other chapters, but change the forehand instructions to backhand instructions. From chapter 2, you can use the forehand game, forehand human ball machine, and five-point games. From chapter 3, you can use the hit-and-get drill.

EXERCISE MAT DRILLS

Flatten the forehand and backhand swing with mat drills. Stack exercise mats approximately waist high, and swing the racket over them. To do this, stand about three feet (1 meter) away from the

4.6 **Exercise mat drills.**

stacked mats and get into a racquetball stance. The stance should put you at the halfway point of the mats at a 90-degree angle to them. From this position, without moving your feet and using only your hips and legs, practice swinging flat across the mats (figure 4.6). If the racket hits the mats, you are swinging up and down. Hitting the mats also means you are using a pendulum swing and not a flat swing.

You can make the exercise mat drill more effective by using the mirror in the aerobics room. Do the same exercise, but put the mats in front of the mirror and swing across the mats. This flattens your swing and gives you instant feedback. This also helps you to visualize your swing. Still another variation of this drill is to practice the drive serve on mats in front of the mirror. An unexpected form of feedback here can be mental. As you begin to drive serve in a game, you will visualize the color of the mats in the power zone of your swing.

OFF-COURT PRACTICE

Use a broom handle for grip change. Keep a cut-off broom handle next to the couch or television. When watching television, practice changing grips from forehand to backhand. Even better would be to use a racquetball racket.

ELEVATED-LEG DRILL

Try this old baseball drill. Baseball coaches take folding chairs and place the pitcher's back knee on the chair and make the pitcher throw. This forces the pitcher to use his back hip. Adapt this drill for racquetball by using a step riser like those that step aerobics classes use. Put a step riser under your back foot. This elevates your back leg about six inches (15 cm) and forces you to drive off that leg and use the backside.

DROP-AND-HIT DRILL

Go to the left wall at the dotted line, about three steps from the side wall. From this spot drop the ball, palm up. The ball must bounce about waist to chest high for this drill to work. You cannot move your feet, but must use your balance (figure 4.7). Visualize cementing your back foot into the floor. Anchoring your back foot and the resulting lack of foot movement forces you to use your backside to generate power. This allows you to strike the ball using power from your hips and legs, rather than your upper body. If you step toward the ball, you will cheat and not use your legs.

4.7 **Drop-and-hit drill.**

ROTATE-AND-PIVOT DRILL

Put the racket between your elbows, and practice rotating from an athletic base. By *athletic base*, I am referring to the stance you begin in. Your feet are slightly more than shoulder-width apart, and your weight is balanced. Pivot on your drive foot or back foot. Because power is generated by your back hip and leg, I like to call the back foot the *drive foot.* For right-handers this is the left leg and for left-handers this is the right leg. This drill keeps the body coordinated and together as you practice the strokes. What this drill actually does is give you kinesthetic feedback so that you are forced to use your body, not your arm or front side, to hit the ball. (The side closest to the front wall is the front side, and the side closest to the back wall in the stance is the backside.)

PINCH DRILL

This drill promotes backhand–forehand footwork and grip change. From the middle of the court behind the dotted line, hit a forehand into the right corner. The ball will rebound to the front wall, to the left wall, and then back toward the center. By the time the ball gets back to the center, the right-hander should have reversed her feet toward the left wall and be ready to strike a backhand left-wall front-wall shot. This is called a pinch shot, and it is advanced. The left-handed player will perform the drill the same way, except he will start with his forehand pinch, which is a left-wall front-wall shot, and the backhand pinch, which is a right-wall front-wall shot. This drill forces students to practice switching feet, grip, and mechanics, all in one exercise.

CROSSOVER-AND-HIT DRILL

In this drill the player steps over with the opposite foot (just like the forehand drill) and strikes a backhand. The player begins this drill in center court position facing the front wall. The ball is tossed to the backhand side. The crossover step should be a healthy step with a left-hander's right leg and a right-hander's left leg. The step should not be sideways, but forward a little wider than shoulder width. This step will put the hips and legs into position to execute an effective backhand.

SHUFFLE-AND-HIT DRILL

The player shuffles her feet and releases her hip. This is much like a shortstop taking a shuffle step before he throws to first. Baseball players learn to take a little skip so that they can load their hips by turning them away from the target. This helps them play more on the throw. This is true in racquetball as well. Taking a shuffle or skip as they do in baseball generates more power. Practicing the shuffle step will greatly increase the accuracy of your backhand and forehand.

BACKHAND SHADOW DRILL

With the racket face toward the ceiling and wrist stiff, lift the ball to the front wall about eight feet (2.4 meters) high. The ball will come back and bounce in the deep court. Practice setting your feet in an athletic base and hitting a backhand. Hold the pose after hitting the backhand, that is, freeze yourself. This freezing will ensure that you are balanced when you strike the ball and on the follow-through. This is an excellent drill for developing balance and getting the feel of the backhand. You should also check to see how your feet are set and if they are in proper relationship to the ball.

RIGHT-TO-LEFT DRILL

Left-handers go to the left side of the court, and right-handers go to the right side of the court. Open the racket face toward the ceiling, and keep the wrist stiff. Strike the front wall about six to eight feet (2–2.4 meters) high in the middle of the court, angling the ball to the other side of the court. Then track the ball on the other side of the court. Take balanced steps to the backhand side of the court and then a final crossover step with the opposite foot before striking the ball. This drill should be done at half speed with soft setups. This gives you time to practice steps and balance. The drill also allows you to feel the turning away and turning in of the backhand. Don't forget to turn away when the ball hits the floor, and then turn into the ball for an effective backhand.

CONTINUOUS-SHUFFLE
AND HIT-DOWN-THE-LEFT-WALL DRILL

This is an advanced drill, and the mechanics must be perfect to execute it. Keep the ball going up and down the wall by shuffling your feet and hitting straight in. The drill is difficult without perfect racket control and good footwork, because you must be in an athletic stance and shuffling continuously. You also must position yourself away from the ball with the racket face toward the front wall, striking the ball in the power zone to propel it up and down the walls. All of this takes great accuracy and practice. I strongly suggest trying this drill only after mastering those described earlier.

5

Serve Returns

To effectively receive the serve, you must adopt a simple mindset: You are on defense. Think of football. Defensive football players are taught to read and react. A football player has an idea of what to expect from the other team, but he can't be sure that this is what he will see, so he has to react to the play. Likewise, the receiver of serve must read and react to the serve. This is quite different than the serving mentality, because the server has quite a bit of time to visualize the serve as well as the return. The receiver may have no time, yet must react to the serve. Sometimes, by reading a serve, the serve receiver may be able to execute more offensively. The object of returning a serve is to gain center-court advantage. To achieve this you must get your opponent out of center court and get yourself there.

No discussion of serve return is complete without touching on conditioning. The stronger your legs and core group (lower back and abdominal) muscles, the better at serve return you will be. I suggest finding a certified fitness trainer or a fitness program in your area. However, make sure you check with your doctor to make sure you are cleared for conditioning exercises. As your conditioning improves, so will your return of serve.

Returning the Serve

When receiving serves, stand a little to the left of center, approximately three feet (1 meter) from the back wall (figure 5.1). This allows a good angle to the served ball and allows the receiver to protect the alleys. Cross over with your opposite foot and shoot. When you take your crossover step, you will find yourself facing, or parallel to, the side wall. This is called *squaring off* to the side wall, because your body is ready to hit the ball (figure 5.2).

When returning a serve, remember the following to ensure hitting the ball with maximum control: Stay behind the ball, push with both legs, keep your weight back, and stay low. In the game of racquetball, *behind* means toward the back wall and *front* means toward the front wall. If the ball is behind a player, it is between the player and the back wall. Staying behind the ball means keeping your *entire* body behind the ball. When the ball comes out of a corner or off the back wall, you must keep your body in back of the ball to strike it with more force. When you get in front of the ball you can only push the ball.

Almost every sport has an athletic, or ready, position. This position simply means that your feet are a little wider than shoulder-width apart, and your hips are low. The lower your center of gravity, the faster you can move. To move forward and back, push with the front

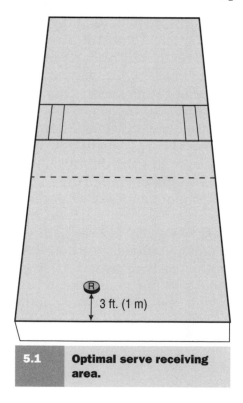

3 ft. (1 m)

5.1   Optimal serve receiving area.

5.2   **Squaring off to the side wall.**

and back of your legs. This enables the hamstrings and quads to work for you. To move laterally, push with both legs. Imagine pushing with your inner and outer thighs, known as your adductors and abductors. Using these muscles enables you to move laterally faster.

In order to stay centered and get to more shots, keep your feet under you. Now grip the floor with your toes. You will find your heels coming off the ground. Stay balanced and in athletic position. It is easy to overstep one's body by taking big steps to pursue a shot. The result is similar to a baseball player running directly down the first baseline rather than curving a little to run through the base. Overstepping slows the player and puts him a step behind the ball, as discussed in chapter 3. This can result in dragging your leg to the next shot or taking a false step. If your posture is correct, your weight is centered over your hips, and you are pushing with both legs as you move.

Players should also keep their weight back for balance and control. When leaning too far forward to make a shot, the athlete loses foot control and is often forced to take a false step. This weight-forward error results in too many crosscourt shots because the player is already leaning forward. Finally, stay "under the roof." This saying helps players visualize staying low. Imagine a five-foot-high (1.5 meters) roof. In returning serve, players must stay below that roof. This keeps the receiver's center of gravity low and enables her to attack the serve.

Serve Return Passes After focusing on the physical aspects of preparing for a shot, the player must next decide on a shot. First and foremost on the athlete's mind are offensive returns. On return of serve, take the crossover step mentioned previously. This will put you in position to hit a crosscourt or down-the-line pass. If you want to hit a crosscourt pass, aim to the center of the front wall, about five feet (1.5 meters) high (figure 5.3). The angle is perfect for the ball to rebound past your opponent and travel crosscourt. This return is called the V pass because the ball makes a V trajectory from your racket to the back corner on the opposite side of the court. If you want to hit the shot down the wall, hit the front wall about four to five feet (1.5 meters) away from the side wall and about four to five feet (1.2–1.5 meters) high (figure 5.4). This will cause the ball to come down the wall. This is called a down-the-line pass, named by our cousin sport tennis. These two basic returns, down-the-line and crosscourt, are offensive returns.

Ceiling Ball When in doubt about what shot to hit, be defensive—hit a ceiling ball. This defensive shot requires the opponent to execute from the backcourt. It also keeps the serve returner from being too greedy and going for too many offensive shots. A racquetball player's natural instinct is to shoot an offensive shot every time. Sometimes

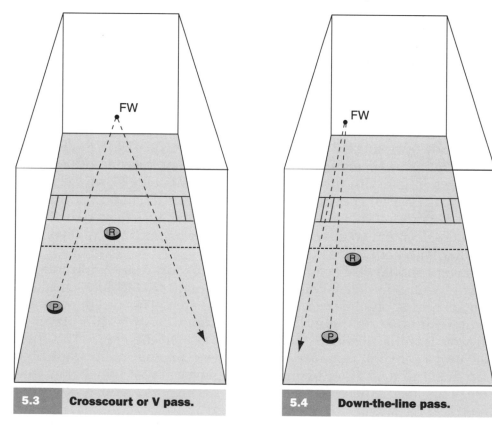

| 5.3 | Crosscourt or V pass. |

| 5.4 | Down-the-line pass. |

the serve is just too good. In that case, hit a defensive shot so that you can get back to center-court position.

Aim 20 feet (6 meters) high to the ceiling to hit a defensive shot over the head of your opponent. The ball will strike the ceiling and then the front wall. It will hit straight down in the frontcourt and rebound deeply into the backcourt. This is the most basic defensive shot. If playing a right-handed player, hit a ceiling ball to their backhand side. If playing a left-handed player, the ceiling ball to the right, or their backhand side, is the correct shot.

To direct a ceiling ball down the wall, aim at the bank of lights that are usually located close to the front wall and about four feet (1.2 meters) out from the side wall. If there are no lights, aim four to five feet (1.2–1.5 meters) out. To hit a ceiling ball crosscourt, aim for the center of the ceiling if you are left or right of center. If you are in center deep court, aiming a little left or right of center will direct the ball toward that corner. This is a difficult shot for beginners. I suggest that beginners hit a straight lob shot. The lob shot is hit just over your opponent's head. The ceiling ball is a better shot because it won't come off the back wall as much as a lob shot will.

A special note to offensive-minded players: Imperfect offensive shots are left up in the frontcourt with the shooter in the backcourt out of position. So do not try to do much with the return. Use the defensive shots to your advantage. Another thing to remember when receiving serve is to defend the alleys. You must intercept balls before they get to the side wall or into the back corners. These two areas are open, and the farther the server moves up, the more difficult it will be to cover these passing alleys. When the receiver plays a couple of steps off the back wall, he can step over and cut off balls going into the back corners.

Stay aggressive with passive serves. If an opponent serves a lob or half lob and you are able to attack it, do so. If you hit a ball just after it bounces, it is called *short hopping* the ball. If you do not have a good shot offensively for an aggressive return, short hop and hit a ceiling ball. This provides more leverage to execute the ceiling ball. If you wait for the serve to come back, two things will happen. First, you will have to take the ball chest high or higher. Second, your opponent will have more time to get to center court. Short hopping stops both things from happening. When short hopping, or cutting off the serve, put your back to the front wall (figure 5.5). This allows you to hit the ball using your whole body, instead of using just your arm.

The short hop is most effective when hitting a crosscourt pass or down-the-line pass. The receiving player attacks passive serves such as lobs and half lobs and attempts to drive them crosscourt or down the line. If a receiver can attack these serves shrewdly, the server rather than the receiver will be on defense. A player also has the choice of cutting off the serve before it bounces. This is done by hitting the lob or half lob in the air, and it is a different skill than short hopping the serve. Remember, the serve must pass the dotted line (receiving line) to hit a served ball out of the air.

Practice your ceiling balls by standing about five feet (1.5 meters) from the back wall and about four feet (1.2 meters) off the left or right side wall. Practice hitting the ceiling two to three feet (.6–1 meter) back from the front wall. Throw the ball into the floor so that it bounces above your head, and let the ball drop to about chest level. Then, redirect the ball up to the ceiling. I tell my students to imagine they are brushing the lint off their sleeve with their hand open. This wrist supination action is what opens the face of your racket and redirects the ball to the ceiling (figure 5.6). This causes the ball to rebound deeply in the backcourt. This shot is called a ceiling ball and will allow the receiver to gain center-court position only if she

| 5.5 | **Short hopping.** |

| 5.6 | **Redirecting the ball to the ceiling.** |

hustles up to center court. If you stay in the back, this shot will not gain you an advantage. Your opponent will have to retrieve the shot, and you will be in great center-court position. If you're having trouble hitting a ceiling ball, simply lob the ball over the opponent's head into the back-court. To do this, hit thc front wall about 10 to 14 feet (3–4.3 meters) high and direct the ball away from your opponent.

Remember that the object of return of serve is to regain center court, so strive to keep the ball out of center court so that you can relocate there. You can keep the ball out of center court by hitting down-the-line passes, V passes, and ceiling balls. All of these shots are great, but they won't help you if you do not relocate to center court after striking the ball. During the rally and in the backcourt, stay away from the ball so that you have more leverage to return it. When there is some distance between you and the ball, it is possible to react to bad bounces and weird hops a ball might take out of the corner. But when you are on top of the ball and too close to it, you will be jammed and unable to make a shot. Flow into center court. Do not run, but move up in controlled fashion. Running hard up to center court makes you susceptible to passes. As a player runs up hard, the ball could go by him and he would not be able to change direction.

Pick your moments for short hopping and attacking. Keep your opponent guessing. When you are way ahead you can be more conservative in your attempts. When you are way behind, try attacking more. If you attack every serve, you may make unforced errors. By waiting for the best chance to short hop, you will create fewer chances for error.

Hitting the Backhand Ceiling Ball When hitting a backhand ceiling ball use the same techniques as a backhand-level swing but angle the racket face upward (figure 5.7). Keep your shoulders level and turn away, and then turn in. Imagine the ball as the face of a clock. Striking the ball at seven o'clock rather than six o'clock puts an underspin on the ceiling ball, causing it to rebound deep into the backcourt. It may be simpler just to hit a little off the bottom of the ball. When hitting a ceiling ball, strike the ball from chest to chin high and in the power zone; let the ball come into

5.7   **Backhand ceiling ball.**

the stance more deeply. If the ball is struck in front of the hitting shoulder, it usually goes crosscourt and is more difficult to control. Keeping the hitting elbow behind the lead shoulder forces the athlete to use the body, not the arm, to strike the ball. This also produces maximum results with minimum effort.

When practicing the backhand ceiling ball, get into the rhythm, turn away from the ball, and turn into it. The turn-away cue is roughly this: When the ball hits the floor, wind up to hit it. This rhythm allows for control and more effective technique. Often the server will hit a great serve. When attempting to reach in front of you to hit a good ceiling ball off a drive serve, open the face of the racket and *curl* it under the serve. This will redirect the ball to the ceiling and use the momentum of the serve to direct the ball upward.

Hitting the Forehand Ceiling Ball   The forehand ceiling ball mechanics are similar to those of the backhand. Turn away and turn in to the ball to hit a good ceiling ball. Simply counterrotate away from the ball, and then rotate toward it for more control. Keep your head level and eyes on the ball, that is, looking right at the ball and locking it into your racket strings. Strike the ball at head height when hitting the forehand ceiling ball. Unlike the backhand ceiling ball, do not let the ball come down to your chest. Hit with a direct overhead delivery, like in a tennis serve. This way you can hit an overhead or a ceiling ball, and your opponent will not be able to anticipate which shot you will hit. Your follow-through should be level. All stroke mechanics should be the same. You do not have to angle your shoulders up. Keep your shoulders level, and angle the racket strings to the ceiling. On the backhand ceiling ball we struck the ball at seven o'clock as we imagined the face of a clock on the ball. On the forehand ceiling ball strike the ball at five o'clock. This creates the underspin necessary to keep the ball off the back wall.

Take it to the court

Think Defense

When receiving serve, think defense. As in the sport of football, racquetball games are won by field position. The ceiling ball or lob shot can be compared to punting in football: They both put the offense on defense and give a position advantage to the receiver. Remember, you have two jobs to do. One is to hit the defensive shot, but the other is to hustle up to center-court position. One without the other is of no advantage! Another tip to remember is to stay behind the dotted line. Do not give in to the temptation to go in front of that line to retrieve a shot; it will open the passing lanes.

Remain a body-and-a-half width away from your opponent in the backcourt. If you hit a good ceiling ball, why go up to center court? Your opponent will have to hit another ceiling ball, and this will force you to go back to retrieve the next shot. If you move only a body and a half away from your opponent, you will not have to travel as far to cover the next ceiling ball. This may seem to contradict what I stated earlier about needing to get back to center court after each shot. That is true, unless you hit a great defensive shot. But chances are you will have to hit another defensive shot. Do not give in to the idea that you must go up to center court each time. This will take you farther away from the defensive shot.

When hitting offensive shots, get up to center court. If you hit a good defensive shot, do not move more than a body-and-a-half width from your backcourt opponent. Relocate to the body-and-a-half position by moving between your opponent and the left wall for backhand ceiling balls. Do not go around your opponent to the right. This will give her position on you and allow her to box you out (figure 5.8). The same applies to the forehand side ceiling balls, as well.

5.8   **Correct backcourt relocation.**

Keep your feet happy between shots. Sad feet stay stationary, and happy feet are always active. Take happy baby steps between shots so that you can adjust to the next ceiling ball. This helps you adjust to each shot and will improve your accuracy. Stay away from the ball, especially when it goes into the corners. You need leverage to return serves from the corners, and getting too close to the ball reduces your leverage.

When trapped, *dink* the ball back. If a ceiling ball is perfectly hit to your backhand, do not be afraid to reach up and try to lob it over your opponent's head. This is a better alternative than trying to hit a perfect ceiling ball return when it is impossible. Another option when trapped is the old around-the-walls ball. Keep the racket high, and scrape the ball into the left wall high. This will cause the ball to rebound to the front wall and right wall high. This is a desperation option when the ball is above your head and not coming out of the back corner. The last option when trapped is the desperation shot. This is just a tap into the back wall so that the ball gets to the front wall. Remember to keep the racket face open, like a frying pan, to get a good angle on the return. You don't have to hit the ball hard, just at a good angle. The frying pan analogy helps you remember to open the face of the racket. Imagine eggs in your frying pan. If your racket is the pan, the strings are open, and you can lift the ball over your opponent's head and high on the front wall because of the angle of the strings.

Keep a wide base when shooting. Keeping your feet wide will keep you low to the ground and allow you to shoot more accurately. When shooting an offensive shot, don't skip the ball. A skip ball hits the floor and does not make it to the front wall. Another thing to remember is not to hit the floor on returns. This causes an unforced error, because you were in a position to make a winning shot but did not. This is similar to the unforced errors made by a basketball player who misses a wide-open layup or a baseball player who overthrows the cutoff man. Make your opponent earn his points.

One of the greatest players of all time, "Dr. Bud" Muehleisen, once said, "Remember, the floor beats most players, not an opponent." If you have a shot, take it. Do not be afraid to hit an offensive return. With a two- to three-point lead, your options open up. You can afford to be more aggressive with the return if you have a lead. This strategy keeps the pressure on the server. The highest percentage offensive shots are passes. You are most likely to win a point from a *high percentage* shot, and *low percentage* shots are those than benefit your opponent. Crosscourts and down-the-line passes are both high percentage shots, because even if you miss, your opponent must track down these shots. The pinch shots and splats are lower percentage, because if missed, they end in front center court as a rekill opportunity for your opponent.

The lowest percentage returns are kill shots. They are the hardest to return consistently because there is little room for error. That being said, remember that great serves demand great returns. Sometimes a player is forced to go for a kill shot off a great serve.

BALL TOSS DRILL

Try the following for solo practice: Toss the ball into the corners and practice different returns down the line, crosscourt, and side wall front wall. As with the serves, work in sets of 10.

SETUP DRILL

A *setup* is an easy scoring opportunity. Use setups to improve your game. To set yourself up, tap a ball to the front wall at half speed. Aim about eight to nine feet (2.4–2.7 meters) high, and open your racket face up like the frying pan discussed earlier. This causes the ball to bounce in a way that creates an easy offensive opportunity. After it bounces once, hit a down-the-line pass (figure 5.9). Chart the percentages in sets of 10 as outlined in chapter 1. For variation, do the same drill, but practice hitting crosscourt passes, V passes, and wide-angle passes. Chart percentages in sets of 10, and when you hit five or six good ones per 10, you will play at a higher level for sure. This drill also works with the more advanced shots, such as the splat and pinch shots mentioned in chapter 8.

5.9 Setup drill.

CEILING BALL DRILLS

Hit sets of 10 ceiling balls to the backhand and forehand. Force yourself to practice offensive shots on poorly hit ceiling balls. Remember to keep your feet moving and to work on the turn-away and turn-in motion discussed earlier.

FIVE-POINT SERVE GAME

The beauty of the five-point serve game is that it works well with return of serve. Set up the rules so you can work on the skills you want to. For example, serving to the right side only works on the return of serve for that side of the court. Switch sides after a few games of scoring on every point with one person serving.

JAM SERVE DRILL

Don't forget to work in jam serves with your practice partner. Attack the ball off the side wall, and drive it down the line or crosscourt. Because the jam serve comes off the side wall, this is a good return-of-serve drill. Your mechanics must be good if you want to cut the ball off when it moves off the side wall. This serve jams many players, because they move too close to the ball when it comes off the side wall. The jam serve gives a player practice returning this serve.

FIVE-POINTS-IN-A-ROW GAME

A variation of the five-point score on every rally is the five-points-in-a-row game, played by traditional rules. This game is won when someone scores five points in a row. If a player scores four points and loses a rally, the other player serves. The first player to score five points in sequence wins.

READ-AND-ANTICIPATE DRILL

In this drill a practice partner throws the ball into the back wall and hits an offensive return. From center court try to read the shot and rekill the ball. Although this benefits the center-court player, it also forces the serve returner to hit a good winner. Score the good shots in every 10 attempts, and switch with your practice partner. This is an excellent drill for reading shots and anticipating. It also provides practice disguising a serve return.

Footwork

The term *footwork* describes the act of getting to the next shot in as few steps as possible and being ready to hit. It is very difficult to separate technique from footwork because each depends on the other. If I had to make a choice between proper racket mechanics and proper footwork, I would say footwork has the greatest impact on your game. You can have lousy racket skills, but great footwork can keep you competitive. However, if you have lousy footwork, great racket skills won't matter much because you won't be able to use them.

Footwork encompasses the speed of movement, the proper movement, and the readiness to hit the next shot. It starts with the ready position. From this position, with your legs under your hips and pushing with both legs, your movements will be efficient and fast. I once overheard a comment about Ruben Gonzalez, the former number one player in the world and the 2002 national champion at the remarkable age of 52. A player said, "Gonzalez never has to get ready to hit the ball because Ruben is always ready to hit the ball." This readiness can be learned through proper practice.

Fancy Footwork

The first step to proper footwork is creating an athletic base. Think of the shortstop who must field a ground ball. He waits with his legs wide and center of gravity low. Coaches call this *athletic position* or *ready position*. In good ready position, which was discussed in chapter 2, your racket is above your waist, legs are bent, and feet are wide. This allows you to move laterally and forward. Lowering your hips allows you to get to the shot more quickly and to remain under control. Try this experiment. Stand up tall and run from the left side wall to the right side wall, a space of a mere 20 feet (6 meters). Now lower your hips and run again. You will gain about two steps of speed by staying low.

One mistake many beginners make is to pursue the racquetball too aggressively. The player sees the shot headed to the right, and chases it. The shot then hits the side wall and comes into the pursuing player and jams her. Remember, the walls are your friends. They will bring the ball back to you, so do not pursue the ball; let it come to you.

The next step to good footwork is to stay behind the dotted line (receiving line) and in the center of the court (figure 6.1). This gives you time to get to the side wall. If you are in front of the dotted line,

6.1 Proper positioning behind receiving line.

you will not have time to set your feet and will end up flicking at shots rather than hitting a good forehand or backhand stroke. Staying behind the receiving line gives you time to get your feet to the side wall, or point them toward the sidewall. As the ball rebounds off the front wall, you must get your feet to the side wall to prepare for your shot.

You must also use a crossover step when hitting shots. The crossover step is executed by stepping over with the opposite leg to execute a shot. A left-handed player who wants to hit a forehand will step over with her right leg to go toward the left side wall. This provides a good base for hitting a forehand. A right-handed player will have to get her feet toward the right wall in the same manner. This crossover move *loads the hips*; that is, it positions the hips to turn into the ball so that they can provide the power for the shot.

To keep your hips loaded, your belly button should point toward the side wall and even toward the back corner at times (figure 6.2). This turns your hips away from the front wall so that you can turn in to the ball with more power. If the ball takes a weird bounce or an erratic flight, you will be in position to strike it with power. Another tip for good footwork is to follow through dramatically with the back hip after striking the ball. This extreme hip rotation transfers power into the ball and brings the back leg into pushing position. Once the foot follows through as a result of the forceful hip turn, push off it immediately to get back into center-court position.

6.2   **Loading the hips.**

Tracking   To open up your stance in order to track a hit behind you, move the lead leg toward the ball by taking a small jab step in that direction (figure 6.3a). Then cross over with the opposite leg. This gets you to the ball faster and puts you in ready position to hit (figure 6.3b). Don't make the mistake of taking a big step with the leg nearest the shot you are tracking. When running toward the ball, always push with both legs, and take small adjustment steps as you prepare to hit. Avoid big steps, because they cut down on movement efficiency. When tuning an old radio dial, people used to take big turns before fine-tuning the dial. The same is so with steps to the racquetball; take big steps to the ball and then little adjusting steps. The happier the feet, the better the adjusting movement.

Ready Feet   One way to improve your game is to have ready feet. On the court, hit and get; don't hit and sit. After hitting the ball, move toward center-court position. This will allow a greater jump toward returning the next shot. When moving to center court, do

Tracking

| 6.3a | Small jab step, followed by crossover step. | 6.3b | Adjust to ready position. |

not sprint there, but rather flow there. For greater efficiency and better returns you should move in a controlled fashion, not at a full sprint. Stay balanced and low. Keeping the hips low to the floor allows you to move more quickly to the ball. After hitting the shot, keep moving. If you rotate your back hip hard to execute a forehand or backhand, your back foot should plant and send you scurrying back to center-court position, in the center of the court, just behind the receiving line.

As your opponent begins to strike the ball, get into a ready position with your feet set. This ready position will allow you to get to the next shot. Anticipate, but do not guess, where the next shot will go. The difference between anticipating and guessing is the difference between expecting a shot and committing a movement toward the expected shot. The simple expectation means you have a good idea where the shot may go, but you wait to see for sure. If you commit movement to a shot, you move your feet too early and may take unnecessary steps. This results in coverage errors.

Gaining Steps   To gain a step, remember to read your opponent's shoulder (figure 6.4). If it's up or pointed to the ceiling, deepen your court position. If the shoulder is down, move up because he is probably going to hit an offensive shot. If the shoulder is open, look for a crosscourt shot. An open shoulder means it is turned so that the chest faces the front wall. If the shoulders are closed, they are toward the side wall or sometimes the back wall. If the shoulder is closed, look for a down-the-line shot. Never take your eyes off the ball; by watching the ball you can get a step on the next shot. Some beginners just watch the front wall and react to shots off the front wall by facing it. These players lose steps trying to get to the next shot.

6.4   **Reading the opponent's shoulder.**

Banana to the Back Wall   Do not overstep your center of gravity. When you take too big a step, you cannot push off the back leg, and instead have to drag it. This limits your power. Along with this, remember to move "banana to the back wall" when you move into the backcourt. Instead of moving in a straight line, move in a slightly curved trajectory so that you can hit an offensive shot. Picture a banana laid in the center of the court; its curved outline follows the path you should use to track balls coming off the back wall and out of the corners (figure 6.5). This gives you room to make the shot of your choice. If you move in a straight line, you will cut the distance between you and the ball, jamming you. You will be less efficient off the back wall and in retrieving balls out of the back corner.

If you move directly toward the ball, you will be too close to it and have no leverage. This will reduce your shot options. A straight line cuts the distance between you and the ball, and therefore takes away your crosscourt and down-the-line options. Of course, a straight line is the shortest distance between two points, and if the ball is not coming off the back wall, get where you need to be through a straight path to keep the ball in play by hitting it into the back wall. Strive to move back to hit the ball at its lowest point rather than striking it out of the air. Advanced players usually execute better footwork and move back to take the ball at its lower bounce.

6.5   **Banana to the back wall.**

Working the Back Wall

Beginners, avoid the impulse to strike the ball out of the air if it comes off the back wall. At first you will misjudge the ball and miss many shots. However, the more you practice off the back wall, the better you will become. You will play better in the long run if you lose a few games while trying a new skill than you would just hitting the ball out of the air. Also, do not turn around and hit ball after ball into the back wall; instead, work on taking shots off the back wall.

You can figure that a racquetball hit off the back wall will land in one of three areas. If the ball hits the back wall eight feet (2.4 meters) high or higher, it will come all the way up into the frontcourt. Position yourself accordingly, and wait to react to the ball with your feet. If the ball hits the back wall between four and six feet (1.2–2 meters) high, the ball will come to the receiving-line area. Move to that spot, and take little adjustment steps to hit the ball. If the ball barely hits the back wall, it will still come out three to five feet (1–1.5 meters) off the back wall. Move to that area, and keep your feet moving. Remember to keep your racket up, and you will improve your back-wall skills.

SETUP AND SHADOW DRILL

Setup is terminology for a scoring opportunity. In other words, you were set up to score a point. Set yourself up by tapping the ball into the front wall, hitting it softly about six to eight feet (2–2.4 meters) high on the front wall. After it bounces once, prepare to hit the ball, but do not hit it. Instead, examine your position, and make sure it is correct. Repeat this process without hitting the ball until you achieve the correct hitting position.

SETUP AND HIT DRILL

Now you are ready to hit the ball after making sure your position is correct. Keep your weight back as you track the ball, and do the setup and shadow drill, except this time you will hit the ball. Try to hit shots down the line (the side wall nearest you) rather than crosscourt. These shots are more effective and demand correct body control and footwork. If you can execute a down-the-line shot, you can execute a crosscourt shot. The same cannot be said in reverse.

SETUP AND HIT DRILL VARIATIONS

All of the following drills work on the proper footwork, because instead of hitting straight to the front wall, you must move your feet. If you do not have a shot while performing these drills, hit a defensive shot.

- Right-handers move right to left at half speed to set their feet and hit a backhand. Left-handers will hit a forehand.
- Left-handers move left to right at half speed to set their feet and hit a backhand. Right-handers will hit a forehand.
- Left-handers work on moving up to back by hitting a ball to the left (forehand) and to the right (backhand) and work on moving back to hit off the back wall or out of the back corners. Right-handers do the same and work on their backhands and forehands, respectively.
- Right-handers work on their backhands on the left side and forehands on the right. Left-handers work on their forehands to the left side of the court and their backhands on the right. The movement is from the backcourt to the frontcourt.

MINI STAR DRILLS

This drill rehearses how to hit the ball in center court. Go to center court, behind the receiving line in the center, and execute a crossover step to the left and shadow-swing. Then execute a crossover step to the right and shadow-swing. Now open up your stance by stepping back with the left leg. If you are a left-handed player, you will shuffle back one step and shadow-swing a forehand. If you are a right-handed player, you will shuffle back one step and execute a backhand shadow-swing. Then take two steps back to center court and repeat the movement to the right. This will be a forehand for right-handed players and a backhand for left-handed players. Step back to center court with two steps. Now shuffle forward and to the left. Left-handers shadow-swing a forehand, and right-handers shadow-swing a backhand. Then back up two steps to center. Repeat the shuffle movement and shadow-swing to the right side, left-handers swinging a backhand and right-handers swinging a forehand. Shadow-step one step back, hit a backhand, and move to center. Repeat this six-movement process four times in a row. These movements will improve footwork and improve cardiovascular conditioning.

LADDER DRILL

Most high school and college football teams use a piece of equipment called a *speed ladder*. It is a ladder placed face down on the ground. Purchase a ladder and a video to teach you how to do footwork drills on the ladder. These drills break up the monotony of inside training because they can be done outside. You can also do ladder drills inside.

BALL-DROP DRILL

This drill rehearses lateral and forward movements. Your partner drops the ball, then you run forward to catch it before it strikes the floor twice. You can also perform this drill laterally. Face a side wall, and when your partner drops the ball, you must use a crossover step and run to get to the ball. You will quickly discover that you must stay low and take big steps to get to the ball.

TAP TO THE FRONT WALL DRILL

Your partner hits the ball so that it lands in the frontcourt. You wait in the backcourt near or on the back wall, then run to the frontcourt and prepare to hit. This drill is great for practicing getting your feet to the side wall and practicing racket readiness. The drill also demands that you keep your weight back while executing the shot, even when moving forward. You may have to move up so you can hit the ball before it bounces a second time. Depending on your speed, increase or decrease the distance so that you barely get to the ball in time. Here's a tip: Stay low, and take big steps for more effectiveness. Your partner can stand to the side so that you can do this drill laterally with a crossover step.

BALL-DROP WITH RACKET DRILL

This drill is the same as the ball-drop drill, except you will be using a racket. Instead of catching the ball, set your feet and attempt to hit an offensive shot. If you cannot get your feet set for the offensive shot, you will attempt a defensive shot. This drill is an excellent drill for shot selection as well.

BACKHAND CORNER DRILL

Your partner will hit the ball off the front wall into the backhand corner, hitting the back wall first. The ball will rebound into the floor and side wall. You now move to the ball from center court. You must try to stay behind the ball and hit a backhand. You can perform this drill on the forehand side also. This drill teaches you to stay behind the ball and familiarizes you with staying away from the ball as you track it out of the corner. Left-handers go to the right corner, and right-handers go to the left corner in this drill.

TURN-AND-FIND-BALL-DROPS DRILL

Face the back wall. When your partner yells, "Ball!" you must turn and find the ball and catch it before it bounces twice on the floor. Here's a tip for this drill: Turn and take one big step straight ahead, and then find the ball. If you don't step straight ahead, you run the risk of moving right or left and missing the ball. This is a good drill for improving reflexes and movement.

Kill Shots and Passes

A kill shot is spectacular and, like the home run in baseball, a fan pleaser. However, the similarities between home runs and kill shots do not end there. Just as striving to hit a home run can get a baseball hitter into trouble, so too can trying to hit a kill shot. When a baseball player aims for the fences, he may hit a feeble pop-up. In much the same way, the racquetball player who tries to kill every shot may make unforced errors, because the margin of error between a skip shot and a kill shot is often a fraction of an inch. Another good analogy comes from boxing. The kill shot is the knockout punch, but the passing shot is the jab. In boxing, managers try to get their fighters to throw combinations, that is, a series of jabs followed by the knockout punch. In racquetball, I want my athletes to do the same. I want them to hit a series of passes, followed by the kill shot. Very simply, the pass is designed to get the opponent out of center court and get him to hit a weak return. This puts the hitter of the pass into center-court position, ready to end the rally. The kill shot is designed for one purpose: to end the rally.

Crosscourt Kill Shot

The first step to an effective kill shot is to let the ball drop. Practice allowing the ball to fall. This lets gravity help you and takes pressure off you. If you strike the ball at the top of its bounce, you must fight the forces of gravity. By striking a ball when it is high, you force it down the front wall where it will rise higher on the rebound off the front wall. This gives your opponent time to track this downward-angled shot. By letting the ball drop and guiding it lower on the front wall, the rebound will be lower and more difficult for your opponent to cover.

Be sure to leave room for error. You do not have to hit a perfect kill shot to win a rally. One of the most frustrating things is coaching a superior athlete who tries to make perfect shots. The superior athlete only has to keep the ball in play, because the inferior athlete will make mistakes eventually. By trying to make perfect shots, however, the superior athlete may make unforced errors and put the poorer player in position to win. One note here: As you move up in the racquetball food chain, this rule ceases to exist. The top professionals are all good athletes, and they must kill the ball in big matches. However, even the top pros do not have to perfect every kill attempt, and there are times in a match that perfect shots are not required, even at the pro level.

Hit in front of your hitting zone for crosscourts, and hit in the middle of the zone for down-the-lines. Remember the power zone from forehand and backhand lessons in chapters 2 and 4? If you hit the ball in front of the power zone, the ball will go crosscourt. If you hit in the middle of the zone, it will travel down the line. Check these points to determine why the ball went where it did.

Crosscourt kill shots are the easiest and most forgiving to execute away from your opponent's position (figure 7.1). Instead of trying to hit kill shots low on the front wall, aim about one to two feet (.3–.6 meters) high to the right or left of center. This causes the ball to travel away from center court and gives you and your opponent a great workout as you both chase shots hit

7.1 **Crosscourt kill shot.**

away from center court. Hitting a kill shot aimed right at your opponent is a very low percentage shot that will only benefit the other player.

You can always use the side walls, especially if the opponent is near a wall, and you have an offensive shot. Aiming for the side wall will put the ball low on the front wall as it rebounds off the side wall. The ball will travel away from your opponent.

67

Down-the-Line Kill Shot

Another option is to rekill down the line (figure 7.2). This is the shot that your opponent leaves up in the frontcourt that you attempt to kill. Your opponent tried to kill it and missed. You are attempting a rekill. The hardest shot for an opponent to track is the rekill down the line. Beginning players get into the habit of hitting the ball back crosscourt, but this gives an opponent more time to track a shot. It is better to rekill it down the line. It is also an easier shot to execute because it doesn't have to travel far. There will also be more margin for error, because the opponent is out of position to cover the down-the-line shot.

The Don'ts of Kill Shots Don't dink when you can rip. A dink is the shot that a player tries to softly tap into the front wall. Do not try finessing the drop shot on the front wall. Hit it hard and down the line so your opponent has no chance to get to the shot. Many close matches are lost because the cute little dink attempt failed to make the front wall or was left up high so the opponent could make a winning shot.

Don't make a shot based on where the ball is. Many times because of poor footwork or technique the player takes a ball at any height

7.2 **Down-the-line kill shot.**

it comes to her and shoots it. Instead, make the shot based on your opponent's positioning. If your opponent is up too close (in front of the dotted line), kill down the line. If he is back too far, hit a pinch lower in the corners (figure 7.3). Strive to let the ball drop lower so that you can kill it.

Don't hit the ball back to center court from the backcourt. This is easier said than done, but hitting the front wall slightly to the right or left of center will angle the ball away from center court, forcing the defensive player to run the farthest distance to retrieve the shot. If you aim for the corners from the backcourt, the shot must be perfect. If that seems to contradict my previous advice of using the side walls, remember that your opponent is positioned toward the

7.3 **Lower pinch in the corners.**

side wall, and therefore, must travel the farthest distance to track the shot. As a general rule, when your opponent is in good position in center court, try not to use the side walls.

Don't try to be perfect on rekills. Rekills from the front do not have to be perfect. First, the player who has just hit the shot is in the backcourt, and, therefore, the farthest from the ball. Hitting the front wall first is imperative. Many racquetball players have gotten into trouble trying to hit a perfect shot on the rekill.

Don't hit the upfront shots hard. Just as the pool player hits a ball hard into the pocket, and the billiard ball rattles around in the pocket and comes out, so too does the racquetball bounce right back to an opponent when struck too hard. Use a normal stroke, but shorten it a little like you would a volley in tennis. But remember not to dink the shot!

Rules for Passing Shots   Remember what we discussed in the opening of this chapter: The kill shot is for show, but the pass shot is for dough. The kill shot is the knockout punch, and the pass shot is the body blow. It is the body shots that bring the boxer down, and it is the passing game that complements and makes the kill shot more effective. Many times the defensive shot opportunity does not present itself. What options do you have if your opponent doesn't give you a great serve? The answer is *not many*. Great returns come after great serves. Often on return of serve you have no choice but to go for a kill shot. Great serves lead to great returns, because there is no other choice for the receiver. Don't be afraid to take that shot on return of serve.

The spot to hit for a good crosscourt pass is toward the middle of the front wall. Aim to the left of middle for crosscourt right. The angle will be perfect for a pass to the opposite side of the court. For a crosscourt pass left, aim to the right of middle. Remember, the spot on the front wall is almost in the middle, just a little left to travel left and right to go right. The basic rule is to use the side walls less than the front wall. From deep court, think side wall only about 30 percent of the time. Any more than that will allow your opponent to play forward and retrieve balls in center court. From the frontcourt think side wall about 40 percent of the time. When an opponent is behind the dotted line, the positioning lends itself to more pinch attempts until the opponent adjusts by moving up.

The shortest distance between two points is a straight line. Likewise, in racquetball the best shot is down the line. Down-the-line passes are the shots that yield the highest percentage and are hardest to defend because the defender is not at a good angle to retrieve the shot, let alone hit an offensive shot. Passing shots wear down your opponent. By moving your opponent up and back, you will have more room for error on your shot.

Although the down-the-line shot is the highest-percentage pass, the crosscourt V pass is also a bread-and-butter shot (figure 7.4). The advantage of this shot is that it provides more room for error, because the ball travels a greater distance. In tennis this is the highest percentage shot because of the large amount of court a player must cover to retrieve the shot. In racquetball, however, there are side walls, and if the crosscourt is not hit perfectly, the shot comes back toward the opponent. The traditional crosscourt passing shots are called the V passes because when you're drawing the angle of trajectory from center court, the shots create a V into the corners on the opposite side of the court. When this shot is executed perfectly, it bounces twice before going into the left or right corner and gets by the opponent in center court.

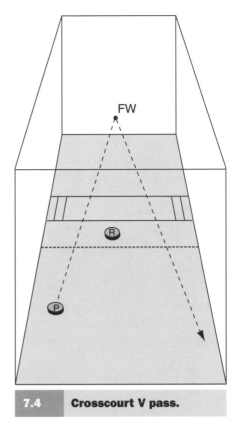

7.4 Crosscourt V pass.

An advanced variation of the V pass is the wide-angle pass, which does not travel to the opposite side of the court into the corner, but goes to the opposite side of the court at the receiving line, thus rebounding behind the player who has center-court position. To hit this shot effectively, aim for the receiving line where it meets the side wall. The shot will rebound behind an opponent in center court, making it hard to track down. This is an advanced shot, and I recommend not using it until you are comfortable with the V pass.

Use the pass in the frontcourt. Repass rather than rekill. Often in the frontcourt a player will get in the habit of trying to kill at every opportunity. Therefore, an opponent will be able to "camp" on the next shot, knowing that it will be an offensive shot. The opponent may also come running up hard to cover the kill attempt. The pass shot will go by her as she hustles forward, and it will be almost impossible for her to change direction. This cuts the open court she must cover in half. To avoid this, repass the shot from the frontcourt from time to time to keep your opponent honest.

You can also throw your opponent off. Vary pass height and velocity to throw off your opponent's timing. Try this experiment next time you play your weekly grudge match. Hit a soft chest-high pass. This will throw your opponent off, and if he attempts an offensive shot, it will result in scoring opportunities for you. The best defense for a softly hit chest-high pass is a defensive shot such as a ceiling ball. However, many players do not have the patience to hit this shot.

Determine the soft spot in your opponent's defense. Then aim for the soft spots in the defender's return-of-serve zone. The soft spot in the passing game is the same as in the drive serve. It is the back left and right corners about five feet (1.5 meters) from the back wall on the side wall (figure 7.5). The hardest shots to get are hit into that area. Legend has it that Mike Yellen, former world champion, used to put electrical tape on the side walls, making five-by-five-foot (1.5 by 1.5 meter) boxes on the side wall about four feet (1.2 meters) from the corners. He aimed for these spots during rallies. These passes are almost impossible to cover, and he invented a new term, the *pass kill*, so called because, although a pass shot, it was as good as a kill shot.

7.5   **Soft spot (shaded box) in defender's return-of-serve zone.**

Points to Remember
About the Pass Shot

A pass shot is easier to hit than a kill shot. Therefore, attempt more pass shots than kill shots, especially if your opponent is in front of the dotted line. Hit passing shots at full extension, hit them hard so that they can get by the opponent, and try to drop your hips lower. The lower the center of gravity, the more velocity your passing shot will have.

If unsure where the open court is, hit down the line. Also try to hit offensively down the line from deep court. Remember that theoretically, down-the-line passes are the highest percentage, but the hardest to execute. A down-the-line pass will hit about six to seven feet (2–2.1 meters) from the side wall on the front wall and pass down the right or left wall without hitting the side wall.

Numerous passing shots are available for various situations. Remember how we hit the wide-angle-pass shot by aiming for the receiving line on the opposite side of the court? Now, hit that pass when receiving the serve by aiming for that receiving line as well. Aiming points for crosscourt V passes during the match are the center of the front wall and two to three feet (.6–1 meter) to the right or left. Aim about five to six feet (1.5–2 meters) high, and you will hit a V pass or a wide angle. Do not hit more than three feet (1 meter) of center on the front wall. Traditionally, players think of shots as the pass left or pass right, but you shouldn't forget the wide-angle shots. A third area for the ball to pass through is the middle. By hitting front-wall side-wall at an angle, the ball will pass into the middle. This is sometimes effective in singles, but more effective in doubles, especially against a right-hander–left-hander team (see chapter 10). On any of these shots, let your wrist roll naturally on the follow-through. Don't force the follow-through; just let the wrist roll over on forehand and backhand strokes, and this will help keep the ball off the side wall. The racket strings will naturally point toward the floor.

The passes will deepen your opponent's court position, so if your opponent is behind the dotted line, do not be afraid to shoot a kill shot. To kill the ball, see the ball at eye level. When you see the ball at eye level, you have let it drop low enough. You have also lowered your center of gravity, which will allow you to hit with more force.

DROP-AND-HIT PASSES

Practice the basic drop-and-hit drill mentioned for forehand and backhand in chapters 2 and 4. Instead of trying to kill the ball, aim for the opposite side of the court into the back corner and where the opposite receiving line meets the side wall. For variation, perform this same drill, but alternate between down-the-line passes, crosscourt V passes, and wide-angle crosscourt passes.

BACK-WALL PASS-SHOT DRILL

Hit pass shots off the back wall. Set yourself up off the back wall by tossing the ball on the floor and into the back wall. On the rebound off the back wall, hit a crosscourt pass, then a crosscourt wide-angle pass, and then a down-the-line pass.

SETUP DRILL

Become a human ball machine. Hit yourself easy shots to practice on. As mentioned in other chapters, hit the ball softly to the front wall, and let it bounce once. The ball should come to midcourt on the right or left. Practice this same drill off the back wall, and aim for the pass shots. The setup for this drill is about eight feet (2.4 meters) high off the front wall, to the floor, and then off the back wall. From this setup practice the crosscourt V pass, the down-the-line pass, and the wide-angle pass. You can hit yourself all types of half-speed setups. This helps reinforce footwork. Hit setups to work on kill shots and passes. This solo practice at half speed will help your stroke mechanics and footwork.

RACQUETBALL/SQUASH GAME

A great game is the racquetball/squash game. Squash is similar to racquetball, but has a "tin" that is three feet (1 meter) high on the front wall. If you hit this tin, you lose the rally. In racquetball you are rewarded for hitting the ball low on the front wall during a rally. In squash you are not. Play racquetball/squash by putting a piece of electrical or masking tape on the front wall three feet (1 meter) high. Any ball hit below this tape is a miss. This keeps the players rallying and working on the passing angles. This is a very tiring game, because players end up chasing the ball all over the court. An added benefit is that they can work on cardiovascular conditioning as well as passing shots.

PASS OBJECTIVE GAME

This is a rules variation game that forces the player to focus on a pass or a kill. In this game you earn two points for a pass-shot winner and one shot for a kill-shot winner. Of course, this encourages players to focus on their passing game. You can also reverse these rules to work on kill shots.

MIKE YELLEN'S DRILL

As mentioned earlier, this is the drill that Mike Yellen used to execute in practice. With tape, make boxes on the side walls that are five by five feet (1.5 by 1.5 meters) and approximately four feet (1.2 meters) from the left and right corners. Aim for these boxes on passing shots. If this drill worked for the world champion, it will work for you too. Play a regular game but score more for shots that hit those boxes.

PASS GAME DRILL

Often a player's killing game stops working. No matter how the player tries, she cannot kill the ball. This is much like a three-point shot slump in basketball. The three-point shooter lives in a world where inches separate hero from goat in a game. In the pass game drill, the player simply tries to pass on every shot. Students are often shocked to see how many games they can win like this, without even attempting a kill shot. The reason for their success is twofold. One, they do not skip the ball as they would on a kill attempt, and two, they hit only one-wall shots. By hitting only one-wall shots, the ball is not in center court off of a side-wall attempt that missed. Don't forget: The pass shot is the bread-and-butter for the racquetball player, while the kill shot is a little extra gravy!

Side-Wall Serves and Shots

Now, after mastering one-wall passes and kills discussed in chapter 7, you must learn how to use the side wall. We have already established that the side-wall shots are lower percentage than the one-wall shots. We have also seen all that can go wrong with side-wall shots as the ball comes into center court. Why then do we need side-wall shots? Because during the course of a game, an opponent will camp out deep in center court to pick off passes and redirect them into the side wall. To keep an opponent honest, you have to use the side wall. The side-wall shots are complementary to passing and one-wall kill shots. The side wall causes shots to take a different trajectory, jams an opponent, or is a counter for the opponent in deep center-court position. The side wall is effective against the player who is slow to move forward. So you may have to use the side wall as part of a strategy as well as part of the natural process of shot selection.

Side-Wall Serves

8.1 Z serve.

Using the side wall on serves allows the server to catch the returner off balance and jam him. The jamming effect is created as the ball travels off the wall into an opponent's body, making it difficult for him to hit the ball when it's so close to his body. It also gives the returner a different angle and causes momentary confusion. One serve that does this very well is the drive Z serve. Hit a drive Z serve by aiming into the right or left corner. You can hit this serve with a forehand or backhand stroke, but most players prefer the forehand stroke. Make sure the ball strikes the front wall about six to nine feet (2–2.7 meters) high and about two feet (.6 meter) from the side wall (figure 8.1).

Remember, it is an automatic loss of serve if the ball hits the side wall first. Because the ball will travel in a Z trajectory, hitting the front wall, right side wall, the floor, and then the left side wall, the ball comes across the receiver's body. This makes the serve more difficult to return. The right-handed player has to hit the serve into the corner, and then step counterclockwise to relocate to center court. The left-handed player is at an excellent angle to hit this serve to a right-hander's backhand. She too must relocate by stepping counterclockwise from the server's box to relocate to center court. In the rare case that a left-hander must hit a Z serve to the right, she will employ the same tactics as a right-hander serving left. She will hit into the front left corner about eight feet (2.4 meters) high, and relocate by stepping clockwise from the right side. The right-handed player also steps clockwise from the right side.

When hitting the Z serve, be sure to get a good angle to the side wall. This is crucial to a good angle to the backcourt. If the ball is hit too far away from the corner, it will travel into the center of the court, and your opponent will be able to attack it with her forehand if she is right-handed or her backhand if she is left-handed. When hitting a Z serve, both right-handed players and left-handed players should stand to the left of center about three to six feet (1–2 meters) to get an angle on the right corner (figure 8.2). If a player is going to hit a Z serve to the right side, he will have to step three to six feet (1–2 meters) from center to get a good angle to the right.

One good way to approach the Z serve is to hit a drive serve into the corner about eight feet (2.4 meters) high. It helps to drop the ball out in front of your body to get a good angle. However, one problem with this type of positioning is that it signals to your opponent that you are going to hit a Z serve, and he can prepare for it. One solution to this dilemma is to hit three different types of Z serves. The first is to hit low to high. This serve is struck at an upward angle into the corner. The ball travels upward as it rebounds toward the back left corner.

8.2 **Left-handed Z serve.**

When your opponent becomes comfortable with the down-to-up angle Z serve, switch to the high-to-low Z serve. This serve is struck at chest level and driven down toward the front corner. If executed correctly, this serve will strike the front wall about six to eight feet (2–2.4 meters) high and rebound into the left corner, traveling in a downward trajectory. It is a subtle difference but very effective. The third type of Z serve is struck at a medium to soft pace, which will throw off your opponent's timing. This serve can be struck low to high or high to low. Think of rolling the serve off the racket face. All Z serves strike the front wall corner and rebound to the right wall about 8 to10 feet (2.4–3 meters) high. Strike the ball deeper in the stance (more toward the midline of your body) on the Z serve to get the ball into the corner. Using these three serves will make it difficult for your opponent to attack the Z serve.

More Side-Wall Serves   If these Z-serve weapons are not enough, two more serves can also throw off your opponents. These serves have already been mentioned, but must be discussed again for use with the Z-serve offense. The first is the push half lob. This serve is hit with the same motion as the drive Z, but instead of hitting a Z, the right-hander pushes the lob behind her. This is effective for players trying to cut off the Z serve. The second weapon is the drive serve off the same motion as the Z serve. The left-hander and right-hander make their Z-serve approaches to the left, but at the last second hit a drive serve to the right. If set up correctly with lots of prior Z serves, the serve returner will have no chance to get to the well-hit drive serve off the Z-serve motion. Remember, only use these serves to keep your opponent honest and from attacking the Z serve. If you use the drive serve and half lob too much, they will cease to be effective.

Another great Z serve is the lob Z serve. The lob Z serve combines the lob serve with the Z serve. It is a soft high serve hit in the Z trajectory. When hit correctly, it is difficult to return. It can be struck with a forehand or backhand stroke. The backhand stroke is sometimes preferred so that the server does not have to turn her back to his opponent and thus can visually track the serve better (figure 8.3). When hitting with a forehand stroke, the server must

8.3   **Backhand lob Z serve.**

turn his back on the ball and may lose sight of it for a second. The object is to hit the corner of the front wall and side wall very high, 16 to 18 feet (5–5.5 meters) high, with the ball bouncing about halfway into the receiving zone where it is more difficult to intercept.

Vary the speeds of the Z serves. Do not hit the Z serve hard all of the time. A soft Z serve with "air" under the ball will rebound high and deep to your opponent's backhand or forehand and give her problems. It is hard to attack a serve that changes trajectory and speed as it approaches.

A jam serve does not refer to a type of preserves derived from fruit. Instead, it is a serve that rebounds off the side wall. It is actually a form of drive serve directed into the side wall at the receiving line. The ball comes off the side wall and moves into an opponent's body (figure 8.4). Because the serve comes off the side wall and jams an opponent by moving into her, it is called a jam serve. This serve is

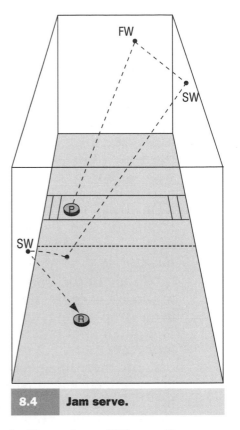

8.4   **Jam serve.**

especially effective against tall players. The ball coming off the wall takes away leverage from the receiver of the serve. The purpose of most drive serves is to put the ball into the corner. However, a surprising side-wall serve is a drive serve that hits a side wall about two to four feet (.6–1.2 meters) from the back wall. This is called the deep jam, and is the most difficult drive serve to return. Because of its angle, this serve is impossible to return if it does not come off the back wall.

The same strategy can be used with a slop lob. The slop lob is a chest-high serve hit from head height or higher. It is a variation of the half lob, and is struck in a trajectory that puts the ball off the side wall and the floor about 37 feet (11.3 meters) from the front wall. This serve is hit in the same spot, except instead of being hit hard like a drive serve, it is hit chest high and soft.

Side-Wall Offensive Shots   Power players who hit straight and hard to the front wall can be countered by using the side walls. Redirecting the shot into the side wall in the frontcourt during rallies forces the opponent to move up to the frontcourt. This makes it difficult for the power player to set his feet. (See chapter 9 for more strategies.)

Use the side wall in the backcourt during rallies. This jams your opponent by moving the ball into her and makes return of serve more difficult. One way to do this is to use the Z ball. The Z ball is not used enough in singles, but used very effectively in doubles. Do not confuse the Z shot with the Z serve. The Z serve hits the front wall, then the side wall, and then rebounds at a sharp angle across the short line into the deep court. The Z ball hits front wall, side wall, side wall to achieve the Z angle. This shot is difficult for your opponent to track down because it rebounds directly off the third wall, straight into her. Remember, the three walls must be hit in the air for this shot to be effective.

The final shot to use during a rally is the pinch shot. A pinch shot hits the side wall about three to four feet (1–1.2 meters) high, and then rebounds to the front wall. The shot will travel away from a player to the left of center if it is hit into the left corner. The shot will travel away from a player to right of center if it is hit into the right corner. The pinch shot is best executed by imagining a box about four by four feet (1.2 by 1.2 meters) in each of the lower corners. Strike the ball into these imaginary boxes for a pinch shot (figure 8.5). This shot is also effective against someone playing deep-court position. Do not hit this shot when the opponent is close to the front wall, because the ball travels to him in the center if the shot is not perfect.

8.5 Pinch shot.

Advanced players, don't forget the splat shot. The splat is for advanced players because it takes perfect technique to hit correctly. To hit a splat shot, aim for the side wall in the deep court. Lean into the ball and hit it at a 135-degree angle (with your racket to the side wall) into that wall (figure 8.6). This causes the ball to momentarily lose its shape. A splat sounds like a window shade rolling up. The ball is difficult to track and return. Splats cannot be hit effectively from the center of the court. They are best executed off shots along either wall. Like the pinch shot, these shots travel away from center court. Some courts have side-wall glass. On the glass side-walled courts, this shot is effective because it is impossible to see the ball hit in the glass wall.

Another trick for intermediate to advanced players is to experiment with shots to the center off the side wall. This jams players, especially tall players with long arms. Imagine a six-foot-tall (2 meter) or taller player. A shot hitting the side wall and coming into him with great pace would jam him in the frontcourt. If he gets in front of the dotted line, or receiving line as it is called, this shot is effective.

Remember the jam serve? In addition to just hitting the side wall, variations on the jam serve are possible. For example, a short jam is

8.6 Splat shot.

a drive-type serve that hits the side wall just above the doubles box about two feet (.6 meter) high and comes across toward the middle of the court. It can be hit to either side, although it is most effective when hit to the backhand side. This is called a short jam because it lands just over the short line, just long enough to be a legal serve. The medium jam hits at about the receiving line and comes out toward center court. If you hit down and into the side wall, this ball will hit the side wall and move back along the wall. If you hit the side wall deeper in the court as mentioned earlier in this chapter, about four feet (1.2 meters) from the back wall into the side wall, this is called a deep jam. The jam and fly is also called a wraparound serve. This serve hits hard and deep into the side wall about six feet (2 meters) high and about eight feet (2.4 meters) from the back wall. That causes the ball to move toward center court at a high speed and rebound away from the receiver of serve. This is a very effective serve to complement the other jam serves and drive serves.

Another defensive side-wall shot is the around-the-wall ball. This shot is hit by hitting a side wall high in the backcourt. The ball then travels to the front wall and into another side wall (figure 8.7). The difference between this shot and the Z ball is that the Z ball hits three walls in the air, striking the front wall first. The around-the-wall ball strikes three walls in the air, striking the side wall first. For a change of pace, hit an around-the-wall ball during rallies. This breaks the pattern of shot angles and momentarily confuses your opponent. Warning: Do not overuse this because your opponent will get used to it. If she knows it is coming, she can cut off this shot in center court.

A third side-wall shot is defensive in nature but produces offensive results. This shot is called the side-wall boast shot. Usually this shot is attempted in sheer desperation, but it is a thing of beauty when executed effectively. It will hit side wall, side wall, front wall, and side wall, and then it will die in the frontcourt. Imagine a pass shot hit down the left wall. The player on the left hits the ball into the left side wall.

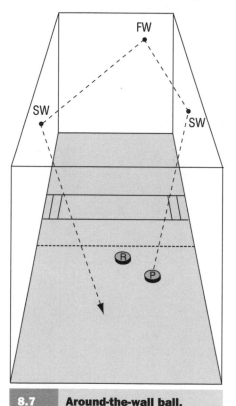

8.7   **Around-the-wall ball.**

Thc ball rcbounds to the right side wall and then back to the front wall. After hitting the front wall, the ball moves toward the left side wall and dies. This is called a boast shot and is used in squash. It is very hard to hit consistently in racquetball, but as a surprise shot, it is a useful tool. This shot is attempted when the ball has passcd the offensive player, who has no choice but to reach behind him and attempt this shot in desperation.

On-Court Strategy

The following are tidbits of information that can mean the difference between winning and losing. First, when hitting Z serves, don't forget to hit a lob serve to the left once in a while and a drive serve to the right from this position so that the receiver does not move over to cut off the serve. This applies to left-handers as well as to right-handers. Hitting only Z serves from this position tips off the receiver about the serve.

Second, remember to strike the side wall on slop serves and drive serves 36 to 38 feet (11–11.5 meters) deep, and continue to vary the angles and speed of those serves to elicit weak returns. When playing the rallies, use the pinch shot in the frontcourt. Let the ball come deeper into your stance so that all you have to do is turn. If your racket is high and the ball comes into your stance, when you turn on the ball it will have to hit the side wall.

Don't forget that pinch shots can also be hit from overhead positions; tennis players will find this a natural shot to execute. Take balls in deep court that are hit over head height, and hit them down into the invisible four-by-four-foot (1.2 by 1.2 meters) boxes in the frontcourt that you aim for when hitting a good pinch shot. This shot can be deadly. Complement the pinch shots by jamming the player in the frontcourt. Hit the front wall, then the side wall, and bring the ball into your opponent. This strategy is like that used by the tennis player who hits the ball right at the person on the net. This jams the tennis player. In racquetball, because we have a side wall, the ball can be hit at high velocity right at an opponent. The tip to remember during a rally is that the wide-angle pass is a side-wall shot. Use it during the rallies.

Z-SERVE TARGET DRILL

One of the problems with the Z serve is accuracy. Sometimes the angle is not tight enough into the corner, or a player can miss the front wall and hit the side wall first. To remedy this, you must practice. Remember the philosophy of perfect practice makes perfect? A suggestion for practice is to put electrical tape on the front wall where you want to aim your Z serve. Practice with a bucket of racquetballs. Don't forget to practice relocation to center court.

PINCH-SHOT DRILL

A great pinch-shot solo drill is also a great drill for footwork. You should stand in the center of the court just behind the receiving line. Execute a pinch shot to the right corner, and then, as the ball rebounds from the front wall to the left wall and back into center, reverse your feet and execute a shot into the left corner. For the drill to work correctly you must start turning to the next shot as soon as you hit the first pinch. You will find that your feet will establish a rhythm after a few shots. You will move in a sequence of shoot, step, step, step, and shoot another pinch to the opposite corner. Instead of shoot, step, step, step, think shoot, one, two, three, shoot. This drill works on pinch shots, footwork, and racket preparation.

SPLAT-SHOT PRACTICE

Splat shots are impressive but hard to execute. Practice splat shots by throwing the ball high and letting it drop to chest height. Then, strike the ball into the side wall at a 135-degree angle. After you become proficient at this, hit a setup to yourself, and then execute the shot. Be sure to work this shot on both sides, forehand and backhand.

BUCKET-OF-BALLS DRILLS

Take a bucket of racquetballs and go to the back corner of the court about five feet (1.5 meters) from the back wall. Throw a ball into the air over your head, and work on Z balls and around-the-wall balls by hitting them in solo practice. Aim about 16 to 18 feet (5-5.5 meters) high on the side wall for an around-the-wall ball. Aim the same height on the front wall close to the side wall, for a Z ball. Notice that the softer and higher the shots are hit, the more effective they are.

REVERSE-PINCH-SHOT DRILL

Work on the angles. Stand in the frontcourt to the right or left of center behind the dotted line, and aim for the opposite corner. As the ball rebounds to you, hit another pinch into the same corner. If you hit it correctly, the ball will continue to hit the side wall, front wall, other side wall, and come back to you (figure 8.8). This drill is great for footwork and getting to know the walls. If you are left-handed and stand to the right of center court and continue shooting a forehand pinch into the right corner, this is called a reverse pinch shot. It is a reverse pinch because a pinch usually is hit with a forehand into the forehand corner, which would be the left corner for a left-hander. You can practice this drill with forehand and backhand strokes.

8.8   **Reverse-pinch-shot drill.**

BACKHAND LOB Z SERVE DRILL

Practice backhand lob Z serves. Although harder to hit, the backhand lob Z is an excellent serve because it gives the server a better chance to relocate and allows him to track the ball better when he relocates. If a right-handed server uses a traditional forehand lob Z to the left, his back will be to the serve receiver when he is relocating. The backhand lob Z allows the server to see the ball and the receiver more easily. For a good backhand serve, hit the ball low and high on the side wall about three feet (1 meter) from the side wall. The high tight angle makes the serve difficult to return.

Z-SERVE GAME

Remember the five-point serve game? This same game can be played with a Z serve. With a partner, play games with only Z serves. This gives the receiver a chance to return Z serves and the server a chance to execute them. The scoring is done on every rally, and once a player has scored five points, the receiver and server change places.

SERVE SWITCH GAMES

Try to use different identities for each game. In one game you are Sam or Samantha Slop Lob. Use only the slop lobs in that practice game. In the next game switch to a Z serve. You are now Zelda or Zack Z Serve. Keep switching your serve identity in each practice game so that you can master the serve. Don't forget to use the Larry or Louise Lob Z identity in a game also.

Strategies for Match Play

Games are won and lost through strategies. This part of the game is probably the last piece of the puzzle to evolve in every player. "Why can't I beat this player?" and "What am I doing wrong?" are questions people ask frequently in my camps and clinics. When asked to describe their nemesis, players often describe their opponents in glowing terms as if they are perfect players. They can't be! Every player has weaknesses. The weaknesses are classified by body type, hitting mechanics, positioning, and mental approach. Many top players have weaknesses in more than one of these areas.

Your opponent's weakness is only half of the story. What about your own weaknesses? Your strengths? If you cannot answer these questions, you will not be successful. You are doomed to failure because your opponent may be better than you in your strongest part of the game. Let me give you a specific example. In my early days, right after college football, I could stay in the frontcourt and out slug most local players. However, one player always beat me. Our matches were close, but he won all of them. Then I changed my strategy. Instead of using my normal shot selection, I hit more defensive shots from the frontcourt. This forced him to move back, and it worked. I had to realize that he was better than I was in the frontcourt, and therefore, I had to get him in the backcourt. I also had to realize that I could not play my normal game. If you are not winning, maybe you should reexamine your game. Often a style of play falls right into an opponent's strength. The types of players and how to attack them are listed in this chapter. Most players are not purely one-category players, but a combination of two or more player types.

Player Types and How to Attack Them

When playing racquetball, you will most likely encounter players of many different body types. Use these differences to your advantage (figure 9.1). If your opponent is big and slow, try to hit away from him. This forces the big slow player to move. Try to shoot the lines to make the court bigger. If you shoot down-the-line passes on both sides, the court becomes bigger because the ball is out of center court. Also, the big slow player tends to rush up to cover center to compensate for his lack of speed. You can pass him when he comes up too fast. Pass from the frontcourt when he moves up too quickly to cover center court. Another tactic favored by the bigger slower player is stretching to reach the ball. Because he is slow, he makes up for the lost step by stretching to reach the ball. Stay patient and keep shooting the lines. This player must expend more energy because of his size, so the longer you can keep him on the court, the faster he will tire.

9.1 Each of these players has a different body type and different strategy advantages over the other.

The fast and aggressive player can be difficult to play. Often this player rides an adrenaline flow and has a burst of energy when the game is going against her. Call time-out when this happens, or retie your shoelaces. Do not let her dictate a fast pace by putting the ball into play on the serve after she has won a rally. Try to slow the game by hitting lobs. A trick from our cousin sport of tennis is to hit behind her. Here is how to hit behind: If the left side of the court is open, hit to the right. The fast aggressive player is on her way to the open side of the court, so aim behind her as she moves. This is called *hitting behind* and neutralizes the player's speed because she must reverse direction to get back and cover a shot.

Another body type is the tall and slender player. His weak area is inside his long levers, or arms. If a shot is hit away from him, he can reach, and not only get to it but also use tremendous leverage against your shot. But if the shot hits a side wall and comes into his body, his long arms become a liability rather than an asset. The leverage factor is taken away, and he will be jammed. Be sure to use the side wall to jam him. Good shots for jamming are down the lines and front wall to side wall, then into the middle of the court. Hit these jam shots with as much pace as possible. The only response the tall player will have is to push the ball back to the front wall.

Playing a left-hander can be a strategic nightmare for many players. This is because many right-handed players attack a left-hander's backhand. Many shots carom off the right wall and bounce into center court to the left-hander's forehand. A left-hander's weak area is often down the line on her forehand side because the left-hander is protecting her backhand, and the angle down the left wall is hard to protect. If the left-hander is protecting her backhand side, then hit a ceiling ball or defensive shot to the forehand side (left side), and then go back to her backhand. This strategy opens up the court on the backhand side. It is a natural response for right handers to hit crosscourt against a left-handed player, and this action brings the ball directly into a left-hander's power zone. Because left-handers play more right-handed players than left-handed, they may see their backhand attacked all of the time. Going to the forehand and directly down the line forces the left-hander to protect that side and opens up the right side of the court.

Another effective shot against a left-hander is one that hits the front wall and then caroms into the left side wall. This shot brings the ball off the left side wall into the middle of the court and forces the left-handed player to use his backhand. If the player is a tall, slender, left-handed player, the shot jams him as well. Here is another fact about playing left-handed players. The right-hander usually serves best to his left. Why abandon that serve when playing a left-hander just because it is to his forehand? I agree that a player should not overattack the left-hander's forehand, but a good serve to his forehand once every four or five serves keeps him honest. Another reason the drive serve to the left-handed player's forehand is effective is because it comes across a right-hander's body, making it is difficult for the left-hander to see it. The right-handed server naturally screens the drive serve to the left. That is also why many left-handers hit drive serves to the right. Their motion screens the right-handed player from seeing the movement.

Mechanical Weaknesses and Strategies

Twisty wristy is one of the most common weaknesses I see in my camps and clinics. It is natural for the beginning player to keep close to the ball. As the player reaches the intermediate level, the ball remains close, and the player ends up with mechanics that drive directly down on the ball. This means the player must twist his wrist to hit the shot (figure 9.2). Still, the player with twisty wristy can be effective if his feet are set. However, since he must still twist his wrist to strike the ball flat, the server must only hit a low drive serve to the side of the court where the wrist twist occurs. Because the twisty-wristy player has a small hitting zone, he will have a difficult time. The low hard drive serve to the twisty wristy is almost impossible to return effectively.

9.2   **Twisty-wristy weakness.**

Watch out for the fist grip. This is the grip our ancestors used on a club when they wanted food. I tell students that if they are ever attacked, this is the grip they want to use. However, this is not the proper way to grip a racket during a game of racquetball. It does not produce much control over the racket.

Think of a child holding a pencil when learning to write. He holds the pencil too tightly and does not write effectively. As the writer becomes more skilled, he holds the pencil instead of gripping it. It is the same in racquetball. The beginning player tends to grip the racket too tightly and in her fist. This grip leads to a racket twist. Because she is gripping the handle tightly with no separation between the fingers and thumb, she must twist her wrist to change the angle of the racket for a more powerful shot. It is also a natural product of wrist supination and pronation during the swing, which leads to unforced errors. Hitting low and hard toward someone with a fist grip causes him to mistakes because his hitting zone is a small. You should also note that the fist grip leads to twisty wristy. You often see both in the same player, although not all twisty-wristy players use a fist grip.

Another mechanical weakness is the *poke backhand*. This is a backhand struck using a grip with the thumb on the racket, causing the player to poke the ball rather than stroke it (figure 9.3). The way to beat the poker is to hit soft drive serves, not hard ones. When returning a hard drive serve, the poker can use the power provided by the serve. But if you serve softly, the poker cannot use the power of the serve, and her inefficient mechanics—poking rather than stroking the ball—will keep her from producing the power necessary to return the shot.

Big Swinging Sam or Samantha is another type of player. This player uses excess motion; her swing is too big. Some players add a nervous racket twist on the backswing, what I like to call a *wavy gravy* backswing. This athlete gets nervous and moves the racket head instead of remaining set and executes a swing and a half—set, wavy racket, hit—instead of simply getting set then hitting the ball. Other players create excess movement with a behind-the-head setup. Some pros teach players to pull the racket behind the head, then swing out and around, but today's game is too fast for this.

Another excessive motion is the body twist. Players do not need to twist or contort their bodies to hit the ball, but some do. I refer to these players as *pretzels*. You can defeat this type of player by hitting the ball hard and low right at her. Remember that excess racket movement causes unforced errors. The same principles that apply

9.3 Poke backhand.

to excess racket motion apply to excess body motion. Extra movement causes unforced errors. Rather than executing the shot with good body posture, the player must untwist her body before hitting the ball, which is difficult.

Poor racket preparation can cause problems similar to those caused by excess motion. But instead of taking too big a swing after racket preparation, this player has no racket preparation. This flaw is extremely common in beginners, who often wait until the last second, then pull the racket into ready position to hit the ball. Of course, this stroke is comprised of a swing and a half instead of a swing. Not only will the player have trouble during normal rallies, but often she will have trouble preparing to hit the ball off the back wall. This swing and a half leads to unforced errors. Again, hit low and hard at this weakness like you would the other mechanical weaknesses of twisty wristy, pretzel, and behind-the-head setup.

Positioning Errors and How to Attack Them

The *up-too-close* player likes to play in front of the dotted line (receiving line), which states to his opponent, "I don't care how low you hit the ball; I am getting it!" This leads to poor positioning because it opens up the pass possibilities for his opponent and does not prevent the kill shot. When the player positioned up close gets to the low shot, lifting it up for the player behind him is all he accomplishes. Attack this player by hitting passes. They will not be able to defend the crosscourt pass or the down-the-line pass.

The *back-too-far* player is the opposite of the up-too-close player. This player gets too far back behind the dotted line and is susceptible to pinch shots. Hitting the side wall is an excellent strategy against someone who positions herself too deeply on the court, because the ball will rebound off the side wall and into the frontcourt. This area will be difficult to cover from two or three feet (approx. 1 meter) behind the dotted or receiving line. Attack this player with pinch shots.

Facing either side wall is another glaring positioning error. This usually evolves as players become comfortable looking the ball into the corners on either side of the court. The player allows his feet to face the side wall instead of staggering them in center court. You can crosscourt pass this opponent all day long because his feet face to the side; therefore, he must move two steps just to get back to where he started. The two extra steps make this player susceptible to the crosscourt pass.

Players facing the front wall have problems also. They are not watching the ball behind them, but are waiting for it to rebound off the front wall (figure 9.4). The problem with this strategy is that the ball does not rebound straight back like it does in tennis. Because the player faces the front wall, she will lose a step getting to the ball. Pinch shots are a great strategy against this type of player. The player facing the front wall will move the wrong way when she sees the ball. If the ball comes into her vision on the left, it will hit the left side wall, the front wall, and go right. The player will move to the left even though the ball will go to the right because when facing the front wall, she will react to where the ball first enters her line of vision. Ceiling balls are also effective against this player.

Do not move off to the right or left side of the court after a shot. This pulls you way out of position during a rally. A player who does this has probably been struck with a ball and is a little gun-shy about being hit again and moves off right or left after a shot. When he moves away from center court, he takes pressure off the

9.4   **Facing-the-front-wall weakness.**

shooter because he is in the shooter's line of vision. The little trick of staying in the line of vision puts pressure on the shooter. If you play someone who moves off to either side after hitting the ball, hitting to the open court is the perfect strategy against this type of player.

Mental Strategies

I hate playing Ms. or Mr. Calm-and-Cool. This player never seems to get rattled. She can be very intimidating because she never gets flustered and never seems to move quickly or in an uncoordinated fashion. She always seem smooth and under control. Try to shorten the rallies against these players, because the longer the rally plays out, the better these players will be. An aggressive serve or serve return will shorten rallies to just two or three shots. Be sure to take your 10 seconds between serves by raising your racket. This will keep your opponent from getting into a groove, especially a time groove; that is, every serve is hit within the same time frame. Make your opponent uncomfortable by using your 10 seconds to receive serve. Another thing Ms. Calm-and-Cool hates is the horizontal game. *Horizontal game* means keeping the ball going back and forth on the court and attacking with passes and one-wall shots. This game is horizontal because you do not use the ceiling; the ball travels back and forth, not up and down, and it travels side to side, not front to back.

Mr. or Ms. Aggressive always presses and is very athletic. Your strategy against this type of player is to keep the ball chest high and in the deep court. Up-and-back and up-and-down shots comprise the vertical game. You should keep the ball on the ceiling as much as possible. This takes away lateral speed and forces the player to be patient. Think of a basketball team slowing the game with a set offense. That is the vertical game. Now think of a fast-break basketball team. That is the horizontal game. So the fast talented athletes should play the horizontal game, and the calculating disciplined athlete should play the vertical game. At the beginning of this chapter I asked if you knew your strengths and weaknesses. This is important, because most players will assume a horizontal identity or a vertical identity based on whom they are playing. As a general rule, players begin their careers as horizontal players and later, in their competitive years, play the vertical game. Obviously, if you can become proficient at both games, you will be a great player.

About Game Tempo

Many players just want to get the ball and put it into play. They want the game to move along at a fast pace. With this type of player your strategy is to slow the game. You have 10 seconds to put the ball into play. You also have 10 seconds to prepare to receive serve. Take the full 10 seconds to serve and to return serve. I liken it to stepping outside the box in baseball. Sometimes hitters will take their time outside of the batter's box, and the pitcher has to wait until they're ready. Pitchers do not like this because it breaks their rhythm. Many of the players mentioned earlier like a particular tempo. The vertical player likes a slow deliberate game, and the horizontal player likes a fast game. Make your opponent play at your pace, not hers. Great players can change tempo to their advantage. In a long match the tempo change may turn the tide in your favor. Be aware of your opponent's tempo, and try to counter it. If the pace of the game is not working, change it. In practice matches work at varying tempos, and observe the effect it has on your opponent.

How do you get better at determining which strategy to use? The following are ideas to use in practice matches. Pick players with different styles for your practice sessions so that you can get a variety of experiences and face different challenges. In addition, use the strategies mentioned earlier to play these different types of athletes.

1. Choose to play against the rabbit, the player who is very fast and anticipates your every shot. This player will help you improve your accuracy.

2. Another player you should find is the left-hander. Because the majority of players are right-handed, playing a left-handed player will provide valuable experience.

3. Play a tall athlete so you can practice jam shots and down the lines.

4. Playing a slow player with excellent eye-hand coordination will help you keep the ball out of center court.

5. Practicing with a player who is up too close or back too far will help you develop strategies against players with position weaknesses.

6. Play the cheating practice players. Every club has a player that nobody likes to play. This player cheats and takes advantage of the rules. Try to play matches with this person; it will prepare you for competition. If the player takes advantage of the rules, remember that when you play him in a tournament with a referee, you will be up four points because he usually steals that many in practice.

7. Take 10 seconds before practicing every lob serve. This is un-nerving in practice, but if it is difficult to do in practice, think of the effect it will have in a close game

Match-Play Strategy Tips

When playing a league or tournament match, or maybe your weekly grudge match, try some of these tricks of the trade.

1. Look for the weak-movement pattern. Does the player move faster to the right or the left? Is your opponent weak moving up or back?

2. Look at the height he hits the ball. Does he like the ball low or high?

3. What is her strongest side? Let your opponent warm up first. She will usually hit from her strongest side.

4. Does the player have a weak backhand or forehand? If so, try keeping the ball to that weaker stroke during rallies.

5. Is he stronger or faster than you are? If your opponent is stronger than you and hits harder than you do, use the side walls. This pulls the power player up, and power players cannot hit the ball hard when they move up.

6. Is she more athletic than you are? If your opponent is a great athlete, hit straight in and down the lines. These shots make the court bigger and harder for her to cover.

7. Mix up the shots. If you get a setup (a shot easy to hit) and you go down the line the first time you get the shot, the next time go crosscourt, and the third time pinch the ball. This keeps your opponent guessing.

8. Slow the game by taking your time on the serve. This is a strategy against aggressive players and players who want to get the ball in play as fast as possible.

9. If in doubt, roll it out or shoot the line. When in doubt or unsure of where your opponent is, go for the kill or down the line.

10. Play the ball, not the opponent. This seems to contradict information stated earlier in the chapter, but this is a good strategy when you're overmatched. The best way to beat someone who is supposed to be better than you is to focus on the ball, not the opponent.

Have confidence in your practices. Take the shots, and don't think in the games. Work on that in drill practice. Don't think in matches but react, using the skills you have worked on. Don't be afraid to make mistakes. The great John Wooden used to say, "The team who makes the most mistakes will win." I know that he didn't want his team to make mistakes, but he did want them to be aggressive and to go for it. To accomplish this, he knew that his team could not be afraid to take chances and be aggressive. Remember, you will miss 100 percent of the shots you do not take!

FLOATING-PASS DRILL

Practice hitting soft chest-high crosscourt passes. This shot is effective against aggressive players, and most players do not practice it much. Hit the front wall a little left or right of center, but softly and chest high, about six to eight feet (2–2.4 meters) high. This confuses your opponent and may cause her to make a foolish offensive move. The correct shot would be a defensive shot, but this soft chest-high shot is hard for many players to resist! If your opponent attempts an offensive shot, he will give you an opportunity for a rekill, or he will make an unforced error.

TWO-SHOTS-IN-A-ROW DRILL

Hit two shots in a row. This is an excellent solo drill and is much like a combination in boxing. Hit a crosscourt pass, track down the shot, and hit a down-the-line or pinch. This simulates game movement and gets you used to thinking about the next shot as you move to the ball.

MULTIPLE-OFFENSE DRILL

This drill is similar to the two-shots-in-a-row drill because it forces you to hit different shots from the same spot on the court and makes the offensive player less predictable. Set yourself up on the right or left side of the court, and practice hitting down the lines, pinch shots, and crosscourts, alternating shots. This will help you get used to using all three options in a scoring opportunity.

PLAY TO THE WEAKNESS

In match play hitting to the opponent's weaknesses is a good rule but not mandatory. Try playing a practice game hitting only to the opponent's weaknesses. Occasionally, there are times when this is not a good strategy in a game. An example would be if a player has a good forehand and a weak backhand. Hit to the stronger side to pull the player there, and then come to the weak side. By hitting to the weaker side only, the ball will hit the side wall and allow the opponent to run around her weak backhand and use her forehand. Because this is not a normal strategy, work on it in practice.

PLAY TO THE STRENGTHS

Now violate the rule of hitting to an opponent's weaknesses in a practice game. When playing someone, why not hit to his strengths so that you can improve your game? Saving the weakness strategies for big matches, leagues, or tournaments is an advisable strategy. But playing to a strength in practice allows you to improve more quickly and gives you an edge competitively.

MULTIPLE-PERSONALITY GAMES

This is like the serve switch games in chapter 8 only we are playing with multiple identities, not just serving identities. Employ different strategies when playing opponents by taking on different identities. In one match you can be Paula Power and hit the ball as hard as you can every rally. In the next match you can be Calvin Control and work the ceiling game and lob serves. By changing identities, you can become a better all-around player.

FIVE-POINT GAMES OF THE MIND

In previous chapters we discussed types of five-point games. Why not put a five-point clock in your mind? After five points are up, begin a new game. It makes no difference if you lost 5-0 or won 5-0; a new game begins. This focuses you on process, not results. You will focus on playing, not the score.

Doubles

Doubles is an exciting and fast game. Because the art of teamwork is involved, many doubles players do not fare as well in singles. A doubles specialist who really knows her craft can wreak havoc on the outstanding singles player. Often in tournaments a team of two outstanding singles players think they will wipe up the opposition, only to be done in by two lesser singles players who team up to make an outstanding doubles team. Why is this? In doubles, positioning and strategies are slightly different. With two people to cover the court defensively, the offensive shots must be more precise. Shot selection is different because the offensive shot is dictated by the position of the opponent on the opposite side of the court more than the position of the opponent on the near side of the court. This strategy runs counter to singles thinking. Many times I see two games of singles going on in a doubles match rather than a game of doubles. Each player plays the opponent on his side of the court rather than attacking the opponent on the other side of the court.

About Mixed Doubles

One great thing about playing doubles is the game of mixed doubles. Women and men playing together can bring a social aspect to the competitive arena and is a great experience when it happens correctly. Unfortunately, a social game of mixed doubles can be ruined by the win-at-any-cost mentality. Here are some rules for playing mixed doubles:

- Don't play the game any differently than regular doubles. In other words, stay away from your partner's territory. Have confidence in your partner.
- Although winning is important, have a sense of humor and enjoy the fun of playing.
- If one team has a partner who takes too many shots, that team will lose to a team who plays as a team. That is because two players have less territory to cover than one player trying to be the hero or heroine covering three-fourths of the court.
- Enjoy the social aspect of the game. Mixed doubles is fun when the four players compete and enjoy the game!

Beginning Rules and Strategies

The doubles boxes are for the partner of the serving team (figure 10.1). The partner must stay in one of the boxes with his back to the side wall until the ball passes the short line. The team determines which player serves first. The partner goes to the box and comes out of the box as soon as the served ball passes the short line. After the first server loses the serve, he goes to the doubles box, and the partner serves. A loss of serve is called an out. The loss of two serves results in the teams switching sides. This is a side out. The team who serves first gets only one server. One partner serves until a rally is lost. After the team gets the serve back, both players can serve. Both players on the receiving team get to serve after they win the serve. The reason for this rule is so the starting servers do not have an unfair advantage of two servers. In the second inning (an inning is when both teams get to serve) both players serve for the first time. Teams can change the order of serve only between

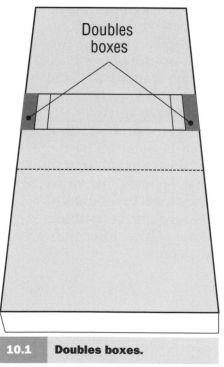

Doubles boxes

10.1 Doubles boxes.

games. In match play games are played to 15 with a tiebreaker to 11. The team who serves first in the first game will usually serve second in the second game.

The player on the other side initiates the serve, then both players can move out of the service zone to play. The player in the box must stay there until the ball passes the short line. Two players receive serve in the backcourt, one on each side. Good racquetball etiquette is to serve to your side of the court. If you serve the opposite side instead, your partner will be stuck in the box and will not be able to come out without being hit. Your partner's proper position in the box is to stand with his back to the wall. The rulebook specifically outlines positioning; if a player faces the front wall to get a good push back, it will be called an out.

For beginning players, two people on a team and four people on a court can be confusing. Remember, any player on one team hits the ball and then any player on the other team hits the ball. Unlike other paddle sports or racket sports, players do not have to aim to alternate sides when hitting the ball, i.e., hit the ball to the right, so the next shot must go to the left. A team may also serve to either side of the court.

Several strategies for doubles play are unique to racquetball. Since racquetball does not require a serve to the right and then to the left, isolating a weaker doubles player by serving to her constantly is a viable strategy in racquetball doubles. In other words, hitting every ball to the weaker player is a beginning tactic in doubles. Another tactic, which is a variation of hitting to the weakest player, is to hit to the backhand. With a team of two right-handers, the backhand player is on the left side of the court, thus the strategy is to hit to the left. If the team is right-hander–left-hander, the backhands are in the middle of the court. Therefore, hitting to the middle is the tactic of choice.

Beginning Positioning

There are two basic ways to position for doubles play. One way is for each player on a team to divide the court into two halves and play an up-and-back formation or a side-to-side formation. In an *up-and-back* formation the front player plays between the receiving line and the short line in the middle of the court (figure 10.2a). The back player plays two to three feet (.6-1 meter) behind the receiving line and covers the backcourt. For a *side-to-side* formation the right-side player plays at the receiving line or slightly behind it about five

10.2a **Up-and-back formation.**

feet (1.5 meters) off the right wall. The left-side player plays at five feet (1.5 meters) off the left wall and slightly behind the receiving line (figure 10.2b). If two players on a team end up in the frontcourt or on one side of a court, they are drastically out of position. Either of these positions is an excellent way to begin playing doubles, and I recommend these coverages to beginners.

Four players in a small area can get crazy, so be sure to call hinders and play stoppage often. Look for your opponent and be liberal with your hinder calls. Be sure to watch for the other team so that you are not hit. Remember, it is better to call too many hinders than not enough.

Side-to-side formation.

Intermediate and Advanced Positioning

As players improve, a variation of both side-side and up-back positioning, the *diagonal* or *sag* positioning strategy, should be employed. In this doubles formation the partner on one side of the court should be up two to three feet (.6–1 meter) in front of the dotted line about five feet (1.5 meters) off the side wall. His partner will be about seven to eight feet (2.1–2.4 meters) off the opposite wall in the backcourt approximately 35 to 36 feet (10.7–11 meters) from the front wall (figure 10.3). Then, during the rallies, the partner on the other side of the court should sag back two or three feet (.6–1 meter) behind the dotted line about five feet (1.5 meters) off the side wall. When a line is drawn from a front corner to the back opposite corner, it forms a diagonal. The players move along this line when they scramble to position themselves. Meanwhile, the opponents try to get into good court positioning. The receiver returning the ball thinks of a defensive shot so that she can get into court position. Her nonreceiving partner must move up to cover the front.

The advanced *modified I* formation is a combination of the side-side and front-back formations. In this formation the server drops into the backcourt of the serving side. Her partner moves out of the box into an area five to six feet (1.5–2 meters) off the side wall just behind the short line (figure 10.4). In this formation this player is at a good angle to cover almost everything up front. The backcourt

10.3　**Diagonal positioning.**

10.4   **Modified I formation.**

player can cover any shot hit by the frontcourt player. This is a great formation for advanced racquetball because it forces opponents to hit perfect kill shots up front. The player staying in the frontcourt is in great position to dig out the ball that hits the side wall. The player in the backcourt can track any ball that is not hit perfectly. This puts advanced teams under tremendous pressure.

Strategies to Beat Specific Coverages

To beat teams that are using certain coverages, you must know the weaknesses in their positioning. Teams using beginning side-side positioning cannot cover crosscourt passes. Because the players are side-by-side, the crosscourt shot is almost impossible to track. Another weakness would be front-court coverage if the players arc side-by-side and on the dotted line. Pinch shots should also work against this coverage.

Strategies for the beginning up-back positioning are down-the-line passes and crosscourt passes. These passes work because the front-court player is in very good position to cover pinch shots or side-wall shots. Down-the-line shots (straight down the side wall) make the court bigger and difficult for those in the up-back position to return the shot.

Attack intermediate side-side coverage and modified I coverage by hitting Z balls. This pulls a team out of position and makes it more difficult for them to cover shots in the backcourt, because the Z ball comes straight off the side wall. This means the player on the opposite side of the court has to cover this shot. Another intermediate strategy to beat side-to-side coverage and modified I coverage is to hit hard and low wide-angle passes. This shot is impossible for the other team to cover well. But beware, the crosscourt wide-angle pass is difficult to execute accurately all of the time. An advanced strategy that works is to hit ceiling balls from one side and then the other. This forces the opposing team to vacate the frontcourt to retrieve the ceiling ball. Because one player is up front, the backcourt player will have a difficult time traveling from one side to another retrieving ceiling ball shots.

Intermediate to Advanced Tactics

Tactics for intermediate to advanced players can be summed up in two words: Keep moving!

Watch the sport of basketball. The team not moving is the team losing. That is because constant movement opens offensive and defensive opportunities. Most of the movement is positioning to anticipate defensive coverages or offensive plays. Racquetball doubles is a team game with the same movement requirements. During the racquetball rallies, positioning demands continuous movement. Each player should move to a spot that complements her partner's positioning. In other words, she should cover the part of the court not covered by her opponent's position.

A good doubles team is always moving because there is always an open part of the court to cover during a rally. How do you know if your positioning is not correct? Look to your right or left. If your partner is along your side, then one of you is out of position. Remember, the pass shot is easiest to hit, and if the two partners are side-by-side, they will be easily passed. Another indication that your positioning is off is that you are stationary and unable to get to shots. You should reposition yourself after every shot. During play the doubles player must perform several tasks in order to cover the next shot: sense where his partner is, move to the uncovered spot (the area his partner cannot cover), and move continuously.

Intermediate and Advanced Serves

Lob serves are good beginning serves because they allow the partner to reposition for return. The middle can also be hit with drive serves from either side (figure 10.5). Z serves are excellent intermediate serves and even good serves to the forehand side. Lob serves to the middle and high lobs that fall into the middle are also effective.

Jam-the-middle serves are special serves intended to cause confusion and to attack the middle of right-hander–left-hander teams. One of my favorites is the overhead jam serve. This serve is hit by

10.5   **A drive serve to the middle.**

aiming for the receiving line on the opposite side of the court. The ball rebounds into the middle and momentarily causes confusion (figure 10.6). Combine that with an overhead Z serve and you confuse the player on the right side. The player on the left can do the same thing using the right wall. For an advanced serve, hit the same serve with a traditional sidearm approach using the side wall, aiming for the receiving line area on the side wall. Spin 'em serves are jams deep into the side wall. The only way to return this serve is to spin around as the ball rebounds out of the corner.

10.6 **Overhead jam serve.**

Pulling the Switch

A player calls a switch when she must be out of position and needs her partner to cover her side. One scenario is the ceiling ball strategy discussed earlier. The team that has to cover these shots may want to switch sides. For example, the player on the left side has just returned a ceiling ball from the left side. The opposing team returns a ceiling ball to the right side. The player in the backcourt, who just returned the ball from the left, yells, "Switch," and the player on the left goes to the right backcourt to return the shot. The partner up front switches over to the left frontcourt as his partner moves to the right in the deep right court. A switch may also be needed to return a Z ball. The Z ball hit to the right must be returned by the player on the left as the ball comes straight off the side wall. This shot will jam the player on the left, so she stays home (up front), yells, "Switch," and the player on the right retrieves the shot. The front left player slides to the right to cover his partner's place as she goes to the deep left court to return the Z ball.

A singles formation is used when a player is out of position, and the game becomes one against two until the partner gets back in position. Sometimes this formation can be used off the serve. The server pretends he is playing singles and the partner will cover anything the server cannot get. The weakness in this formation is that only one player must cover a shot hit by two players. The trick is for the singles player to hit a defensive shot so that his partner can get back into center-court position as quickly as possible. If you take an offensive shot, it is still you versus two opponents, but if you hit a defensive shot to let your partner get back into position, it is once again two-versus-two.

The partner-in-the-corner formation is the same as the singles formation, except that it is not a tactic to be used merely when a player is out of position, but employs a one-against-two strategy to be used only in dire emergency situations, such as the finals of a tournament when one partner is sick or injured. The other player would then try to play one-against-two to win the match (figure 10.7). Sometimes you will see this foolishly done in mixed doubles. It almost never works.

Occasionally, a team may use an I formation to receive serve. Sometimes a partner may be hurt or just plain overmatched. If you are able to check your ego at the door and want to win, you may allow your partner to receive serve. The partners line up behind each other in center court and at the serve break for one side or the other. The designated serve returner goes to the ball while the other partner heads for the frontcourt. The I formation, the partner in the corner, and the modified I are low-percentage coverages and usually would be used in cases of injury to one player, extreme weakness in return of serve in one player, or physical mismatch against the player on one side. Because these formations depend on surprise, the experienced team can readily attack these coverages.

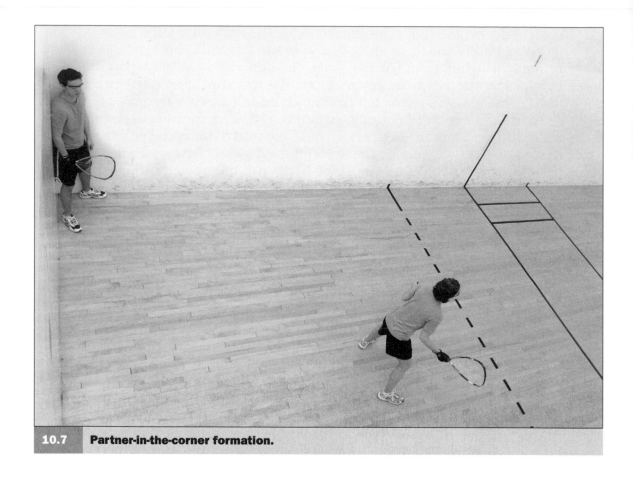

10.7 | **Partner-in-the-corner formation.**

Rules for Successful Doubles

I have seen many teams unable to master the mental approach to doubles. The weaker partner needs confidence. Therefore facial expressions of exasperation and oral berating such as, "How could you have missed that shot?" from the other partner almost always lead to nervousness and a lower level of execution. Don't undermine your own team by criticizing your teammate. Instead, counter those actions with the simple response, "Nice try. That's the shot to go for. Keep taking it." And one of my favorites, "That's okay, that was my fault," works too. This takes pressure off your partner, and allows him to stay loose.

Each team should have a captain. Usually this evolves naturally, and the more experienced player becomes the captain. This player may make most of the calls during the rallies. The calls should be simple, such as, "I got it," "You take it," and "Switch," if partners switch sides. The captain also is the strategic superior on the team and calls for strategy changes, serves to use, and positioning changes as the match unfolds.

If both players call a ball, the forehand player has priority. Usually this occurs in the middle of the court with a right-hander–right-hander team or a left-hander–left-hander team. Because the mechanics of the forehand dictate more leverage, the forehand player takes the shot. This is crucial, because during the rallies, a backhand does not have the leverage of a forehand. I have seen many players almost throw their arm out of the shoulder socket when the backhand player stole the forehand shot, and the forehand player *whiffed* (completely missed) the ball because the backhand partner had already struck it. I recommend that beginners call more shots. As they become more proficient they may not have to call as many shots. The irony is that more advanced players call for more shots and coverages than beginners, because they want to take no chance of a miscommunication. Beginners can learn from this approach. Bottom line: You cannot call for too many shots, but you can err by not calling for enough.

When playing in frontcourt, let some balls go, especially those you cannot take a good shot at. Your partner is covering you and may have a better angle. However, this takes experience, so don't be afraid to try it in practice. Eventually you will learn to tell where your partner is playing and learn which angled shots to midcourt to let go. The player up front must let some balls go when the backcourt opponent hits passes. Rather than reaching out and stabbing balls, a player may let the ball go and let her partner get the shot as it travels into the backcourt. I should note here that this is a general rule. Some players are almost total frontcourt players. That is they can do things in the frontcourt with the ball about chin high that the average player cannot. Those players get more shots up front. But generally speaking, trying to make an offensive shot when your opponent hits pass shots to the frontcourt will only result in a weak shot that a sets the stage for your opponents to win.

Do not serve your partner's side of the court. This is an excellent way to end a friendship and partnership in doubles. If you serve the ball to your partner's side, she cannot get out of the box without being in the way of the backcourt opponent's shot. So you have to play one player against two, and your partner most likely will get hit because she is in the line of fire. A partner gets mad when you serve her side, and she gets whacked in the back because she cannot get out to relocate to court position. Save your partner. Serve only your side.

Earlier I mentioned isolating the weaker player as a beginning strategy. This works at every level. In advanced play there are opportunities to keep serving the weaker player even after one server has lost his serve. Lets say the weaker opponent is on the left. Your partner on the left serves the weak side and scores two points before she loses the serve. Then it is your turn to serve. Because you shouldn't serve to your partner's side, the player on the right would normally serve to the strong opponent on the right. Why not switch sides after your partner loses her serve so that both of you get to serve to the weaker player? You can switch back after the serve during the rally at the first opportunity.

Another rule to remember is this: Do not pick your partner by whom you like best; pick the partner who complements your skills. If you are slow, pick someone fast. If you are good up front, pick someone good in the backcourt. If your mentality is fire, find someone whose mentality is ice. The best doubles teams usually have one emotional and one logical player. A team of two emotional players leads to rushing shots and not thinking through a tough situation. A team with two nonemotional players leads to lost scoring opportunities because they may not be aggressive enough. In key moments in competition one player can calm another, or conversely fire him up.

Doubles Strategies and Shots

Use ceiling ball shots and defensive shots, especially on return of serve. Doubles is a game of positioning. The team with the best position wins. Usually off the serve, a defensive shot is best so that the receiving team can regain position. Remember, if you try an offensive shot from the backcourt, it must be perfect, because you have two people in the front to cover the shot. And remember this: With two people covering an offensive shot, strive not to take that offensive shot from the backcourt. Instead look for a wide-angle pass, a crosscourt pass, or a defensive shot.

Practice the Z ball. The Z ball hits three walls in the air and is an excellent doubles shot, because it forces the person on the opposite side of the court to retrieve the ball. If the ball comes high off the front wall to the right wall, and then travels to the left wall, as a general rule, only the player on the right will be able to return the shot, because the ball will travel straight off the left wall. This means the player on the right must travel all the way to the left to return the shot. This creates opportunities for winning rallies, because the opponents are pulled out of position. This is an advanced shot, so be sure to practice it before trying it in a match.

A variation of the Z ball is the around-the-wall ball. This strikes side wall, front wall, and side wall, in the air. It also is a good doubles shot, but is not as effective as the Z ball because it travels through center court. The Z ball does not. When this shot travels through the frontcourt, a good team will cut off this shot up front. But if you use this shot sparingly, it may take your opponents by surprise and prevent the frontcourt cutoff.

Crosscourt passes are a good strategy for doubles unless playing a left-hander–right-hander team. With a team of two right-handers or a team of two left-handers, one player must cover the backhand side, which is susceptible to crosscourt passes, because the back-hand player does not have an angle on the wide-angle pass to cut it off. The wide-angle pass is definitely the weak part of a doubles team's zone (figure 10.8a).

When playing a left-hander–right-hander team, jam them in the center, where the backhands are. The weak part of the left-hander–right-hander team is in the middle. To jam them, aim for the side wall and bring the ball into center court (figure 10.8b). Instead of hitting crosscourt, this can be achieved by hitting the front wall, then side wall, thus bringing the ball into the middle. Players will be forced to flick their backhands to hit shots off the side wall into the middle.

Good advice for advanced players is to vary your serves. Switch the angles on Z serves. Hitting Z serves at two or three different angles keeps the opponent from returning the serve as effectively. Mix up the serves from lobs to Z serves, and throw in a few drive serves. Also be aware of your position during the rallies. If the ball is deep right, the right-side player should be deep, and if the ball is deep left, the left-side player should be deep. Conversely, the other partner covers the front just behind the short line and five feet (1.5 meters) off the side wall.

Sometimes a reverse pinch from the frontcourt is helpful. A re-verse pinch shot is hit by a right-hander from the right into the left corner. A left-handed player hits a forehand reverse pinch into the right corner with her forehand. In singles the reverse pinch is not effective, because the ball must travel the greatest distance to its target in the frontcourt. In doubles it is a great shot because it is farther away from the opponent's up-front player. It is also a great shot because the opponent's view of the side of the court the ball comes to will be temporarily blocked. (If a right-handed player hits this forehand shot, the ball comes to the right, and if a left-hander hits it, the ball travels to the left.). The ball comes toward the player who hit the shot. The player behind him cannot see the ball because the shooter's body blocks the shot.

Don't skip the ball. A skip shot hits the floor before it hits the front wall, which results in a loss of point or serve. This is what we call

Doubles Team Weaknesses

10.8a Wide-angle pass to the weak area of a right-hander–right-hander team.

10.8b Wide-angle pass to the weak area of a left-hander–right-hander team.

an unforced error. Good doubles players know that skipping a shot is one of the worst things they can do. Two players can retrieve a shot, but nobody can retrieve a skip. It is an instant point with no pressure put on the other team and a doubles no-no for sure.

Speaking of no-nos, staying against the wall is one of the biggest in doubles. Many players have a tendency to hang on the side wall. During rallies the player on the wall has no place to go. Because there is no place to go, the players get trapped on the wall where they could be struck by the ball. This ends the rally, and the team getting hit loses the point or the serve. Another problem with hanging on the walls is that the player on the wall gets jammed and cannot make a shot traveling between the player and the wall.

Give it a go

SERVE PRACTICE

By yourself, practice doubles serves. Hit the overhead jams and some of the specialty serves discussed in this chapter. As in the singles serves, chart the percentage of successful serves by completing sets of 10 and marking the good serves.

REFLEX DRILLS

In the frontcourt, in front of the receiving line, hit ball after ball as fast as you can. In baseball this is called *pepper* with two players bunting the ball to each other to develop soft hands. The term *soft hands* refers to a baseball player who can glove a hard-hit ball softly. This same term applies to racquetball players who can take a hard-hit ball and redirect it softly into the corners of the frontcourt. In this drill the player keeps hitting as hard as she can into the front wall and blocking that shot back with a shortened swing. The way to shorten the swing is to stop it short of the follow-through. This is important in the frontcourt because a big follow-through keeps the player from getting into position for the next shot. This drill also works well with a partner on the other side of the court. Start the partner drill by trying to hit the ball past your partner on the other side of the court. The partner must block the shot and return the ball to you. This creates short swings and fast reflexes.

CEILING BALL RALLY DRILL

Practice hitting ceiling balls from both sides of the court (figure 10.9). In doubles there will come a time when ceiling ball rallies will win the day. Make sure you and your partner can hit effective ceiling balls. Try to hit 10 in a row, and then hit a crosscourt pass or wide-angle pass to the other side.

10.9　**Ceiling ball rally drill.**

Z-BALL DRILL

One solo drill for doubles play is to hit Z balls from the front and backcourt. Notice that the softer the Z ball is hit, the harder it is to return. Aim for a point high on the front wall corner within four feet (1.2 meters) of the corner. The ball will hit the other wall high and rebound to the opposite wall. This is a great shot for doubles as previously explained.

ONE VS. TWO GAME

Many times three people show up to practice. This is not enough for doubles, so one person must sit out and wait through games. The one vs. two game eliminates this problem and allows two players to practice doubles skills, while the other works on his singles game. Each player serves once, making it very challenging for the singles player because he gets only one serve to the other team's two. Play regular rules and a great workout will result.

PLAY DOUBLES

The best way to practice doubles is to play doubles. Find differ-ent partners, and practice positive comments. Nice shot, nice try, my fault, and keep shooting are all positive comments. Do not use negative comments or body language. Also, make your shot based on your opponent's positioning on the opposite side of the court, not by your opponent's positioning on your side. Because doubles is a team endeavor, many players never really learn how to play this game. This is too bad. It not only makes the singles game better, but also is fun. The rallies are longer and more exciting because two people play two. Another advantage is that it gives women a great chance to compete directly with men in mixed doubles. Try this game and have some fun!

Shot Selection and Location

Imagine watching a basketball game. One team brings the ball down the court, shoots a three-point shot, and it is good. Watch the tendency of the opposing team to bring the ball downcourt and try the same shot. Why? They attempt that shot because they want to show the other team that they can make it too. If the latter team had been patient and moved the ball around, they would have gotten a better shot. Racquetball is no different, and shot selection is the last piece of the racquetball puzzle. It is often what makes or breaks a player. It is possible to win without good shot selection, and in recent years at the professional level players have won tournaments with average shot-selection skills. If a beginning player matches up well with her adversary, she can win with poor shot selection. If one player hits with more power, and the other player cannot handle the power, then poor shot selection may not be a factor. However, as the player moves up the food chain of racquetball excellence, and is evenly or, in some cases, overmatched, shot selection determines more and more wins and losses.

Basic Rules of Shot Selection

A player can do everything right but still lose if he has no concept of shot selection. The simplest explanation of shot selection is to "hit them where they ain't." Of course, the open court is the area to go to, but another part of this concept is to use defensive shots when no offensive opportunity is available. When players try to force an opportunity that does not exist, they make mistakes. Here's a more apt description of shot selection: Hit to the open court when your feet are set, but if you can't set your feet, hit a defensive shot. Here are the rules for shot selection:

■ Be more offensive-minded on the serve. If you skip the ball during a rally and you are serving, you only lose the serve. You can take more chances because you will only lose the serve. If you skip the ball-receiving serve during a rally, you lose a point. Getting the serve back becomes paramount to winning racquetball, because without the serve, you cannot score the points.

■ If you don't have a shot, go to the ceiling. Don't try to make something out of nothing. If off-balance or out of position, don't try to make the low-percentage shot. Make a defensive shot instead. A good rule is to hit the ceiling ball when you cannot set your feet, or if the ball is chest high or higher. If you were to try an offensive shot, you would hit a skip ball on the floor, or you would hit an easy scoring opportunity for your opponent.

■ Be defensive-minded on return of serve. The server should be in better position than the receiver. Therefore, unless you have a perfect shot opportunity when returning the serve, it is better to go to the ceiling to be safe. To determine whether you have a good scoring opportunity, look to your feet. If you can set both feet, balance up with both feet in a good stance, then shoot the ball. If this is not possible, hit a defensive shot.

■ Hit to the brown. In football, running backs are taught to look for the green. I am not talking about money, but open field. This helps young players determine where on the football field to run. Looking for the green of the open field is an easy way for the back to determine which way to run. On the racquetball court the brown of the court floor tells the offensive player which shot to attempt. The open part of the brown floor will signal where to shoot.

■ Keep your body between your opponent and the ball. This causes your opponent to travel the greatest distance and also legally screens the ball much of the time. Your opponent must track the ball across your body.

■ A one-wall shot is a higher percentage than a two-wall shot. Because the ball will not be in center court, it less likely that your opponent will hit the shot. If you hit just the front wall, it is difficult to get the ball to center court. When the ball strikes the front wall and side wall, or the side wall and front wall, the ball goes toward the center court. And, if the ball is in center court, you will not be. You will have to clear the area to give your opponent the shot. Therefore, two unfortunate things will happen—you will be out of position, and your opponent will be in position to make an offensive shot in the frontcourt. So shoot straight in as much as possible.

■ Use pass shots. Admittedly, the kill shot is a spectacular shot and has been described as the home run of racquetball; however, it is impossible to win if you shoot every ball. The passing shots set up good kill opportunities. Only when an opponent plays very deep in center court will the kill shot be more effective. Remember, it is harder to hit a kill shot than a pass shot.

Offensive Shot Selection

Situation: The opponent is up too close to the front wall.

Solution: Pass down the line and crosscourt. The receiving line is 24 feet (7.3 meters) from the front wall, and when a player gets in front of that line, he opens up the entire court for passing (see positioning in chapter 3). *Down the line* is terminology for shooting up and down the side walls and comes from our cousin sports tennis and squash. Down the line simply means a passing shot about two to four feet (.6–1.2 meters) from the wall, traveling along the wall. Because the shortest distance between two points is a straight line, this is an effective shot and almost impossible for someone too close to the front wall to return. This is what we call *using the lines.* Another effective strategy is to go crosscourt with a passing shot. This shot is hard to cover when the player is too close to the front wall. Better than the crosscourt is the wide-angle pass, which hits the side wall at an area where the receiving line meets the side wall. This causes the shot to rebound behind the player too close to the front wall.

Situation: The opponent is to the right or left of center court.

Solution: Hit a V pass to the opposite side of the court. A V pass travels into the corner on the opposite side of the court in a V trajectory. The shot hits the front wall to the right or left of center and travels into the deep-court corner on the right or left. If the opponent is right of center court, the shot goes to the left. If the opponent is to the left of center court, the shot goes to the right corner (figure 11.1). This forces your opponent to travel the greatest possible distance, and chasing shot after shot crosscourt will wear him down.

11.1   **V pass with opponent to left of center court.**

Situation: The opponent is in deep center-court position behind the dotted line.

Solution: Hit pinch shots to put the ball in the frontcourt. Your opponent will have to move forward to cover this shot. Because your opponent is behind the dotted line, this creates the farthest distance for him travel. An added bonus is that it is difficult for your opponent to set his feet while moving forward. Remember that racquetball players develop laterally the more they play, and most players have a hard time moving forward, which makes the pinch shot very effective in this situation. Hitting a one-wall shot in this situation will allow your opponent to defend it well from deep in center court.

Splat shots are also difficult to cover. The splat shot hits the side wall deep in the backcourt, but because it rebounds low off the side wall into the front wall in the frontcourt, it produces the same result as the pinch shot. A down-the-line pass is the third option in this situation. Even though the opponent is deep, the angle is difficult for the opponent to return.

Your fourth choice is a wide-angle pass, because it will kick off the side wall and rebound behind the center-court position. This is the most difficult pass to perform and thus, belongs at the bottom of the shot selection list when the opponent is in deep-court position (figure 11.2). It must be executed perfectly to pass behind a player in deep court.

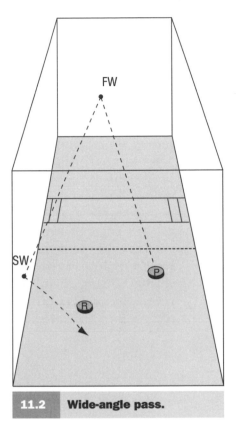

11.2 **Wide-angle pass.**

Defensive Shot Selection

Situation: You are not sure which shot to attempt from the backcourt.

Solution: This situation calls for a ceiling ball. When in doubt, flicking the ball to the ceiling prevents an unforced error. More important, it allows you to regain center-court position. The odds then are in your favor, because your opponent will not be in center-court position. The second option in this situation is a Z ball, which may take an opponent by surprise. A third option is an around-the-wall ball. This also is a difficult shot to respond to offensively.

Situation: You are trapped in the backcourt.

Solution: If you are a right-handed player trapped in the back left corner on a ball that hits the left wall, do not back out toward the middle of the court to attempt a backhand return. Instead, spin around in a counterclockwise direction, and hit a forehand as the ball rebounds out from the left corner. This provides leverage down the left wall and more offensive opportunities. A left-handed player would be trapped in the right corner, and the ball would rebound out toward the center of the court from the corner. To back up on this shot and use a backhand leads to defensive shots and poor returns. The forehand out of the corner gives an athlete plenty of leverage on the shot.

Situation: You are receiving a serve.

Solution: When receiving a serve, remember that you are on defense. If you don't have a good shot, you must hit a defensive shot. This is much like punting on fourth down in football because you are trying to regain court position. Do not decide which shot you are going to make; instead, react to the serve. If it is a lousy serve, take an offensive shot. However, think defense because an unforced error off return of serve results in points. Another thing to remember on return of serve is, don't always hit a ceiling ball down the left or right wall. Opponents are often good at hitting splat shots along the side walls. Hitting a ceiling ball down the side wall gives these players more offensive opportunities. When you hit a ceiling ball to the center of the court, it takes away the splat angle (figure 11.3).

11.3 **Ceiling ball hit to middle court.**

Situation: Your opponent is hitting Z serves to you.

Solution: The Z serve can be very effective, especially if the serve receiver has footwork deficiencies. If the right-handed athlete steps over sideways with her right leg to return a Z serve left, she will not be effective because she has no base beneath her to return serve. The left-handed player would step over in a shallow manner with her left leg. The tendency of the receiver is to hit the side wall on the return. Therefore, you should use the same strategy against the Z serve that you use to combat the splat-shooting player. Hit a ceiling ball into the middle of the court. If you try to hit a ceiling ball down a wall off a Z serve, you may hit the side wall, and when the ball pops out, your opponent will have a good shot. If you hit a ceiling ball in the middle of the court and you make a mistake, the ball will come down the wall. If you aim down the side wall and make a mistake, it will be a setup for your opponent.

Another advantage to returning with a ceiling ball down the middle of the court is that the ball will go directly over the server's head. Your opponent will have trouble relocating after the serve because momentum will carry a right-handed player toward the right wall, and the ceiling ball will go directly over his head. The left-handed player's momentum will carry him toward the left wall, and he will have the same problem relocating after the serve.

Matching Your Opponent

Situation: You are playing a fast lateral-moving opponent.

Solution: When playing a fast lateral-moving player, hit behind her instead of aiming for the open part of the court. Let's say the right side of the court is open. The fast player will anticipate the opening and get there with no problem. That is when you want to hit behind her. Because she has already taken off to cover the right side, she will have to stop, change directions, and go back to the left. This reversal will slow your opponent.

Situation: You are playing a hard-hitting opponent.

Solution: When playing a hard-hitting power player, use the side walls. As mentioned earlier, when a power player sets his feet, he can hit with force. But if you can take that power shot and redirect the ball into a side wall, you will force him to move up, which limits his power.

Situation: You are playing a strong frontcourt player.

Solution: The strong frontcourt player seems to rekill everything. This player has good reflexes, and rekilling the ball is how she makes points. If playing a strong frontcourt player, keep her in the backcourt with ceiling balls and specialty shots such as the Z ball and around-the-wall ball. This type of player will get frustrated being in the backcourt and probably not be as effective as she is in the frontcourt.

Situation: You are unsure of your opponent's strengths or weaknesses.

Solution: The ideal solution is to scout your opponent. Determine where they score most of their points and where they like the ball. Also try to determine which part of the court they have the most trouble scoring from. Divide the court into six areas by drawing three evenly spaced vertical lines from the front wall to the back wall. The receiving line will intersect these three lines and divide the court into six parts: the front three and the back three. The front three boxes will be bigger. Your opponent will have trouble scoring from one or maybe two of these areas. Likewise, find your opponent's favorite section of the court. Then try not to put the ball there, especially in crucial points in the match. At crucial times, the ball should be in the weakest area, because you want your opponent to respond to you with his weakest shot, not his strongest.

Let's suppose you do not have a chance to scout your opponent. How do you determine her weak area? Here is a little trick: Before the match starts, be the second player to the court. The first player on the court usually goes to her strongest shot area to warm up. There are other telltale signs. Some players take backhand shots on their forehand side, while others take forehand shots on their backhand side. That tells you that they have more confidence in their backhand or forehand. Obviously, you want to keep the ball away from their stronger side.

Situation: Your opponent guesses where you are going with your shots.

Solution: Mix up your shot pattern. Try to vary them. Remember the multiple offense drill from chapter 9? That drill teaches you not to take the same shot from the same spot. If you shoot down the line on the first forehand opportunity, go crosscourt on the second, and pinch on the third. By varying your shot selection you become unpredictable. This may contradict proper shot-selection strategy at times, but you need to vary your shots off setups if your opponent anticipates what you're doing. Be sure to vary these shots in practice so that it becomes second nature in tournament play.

VIDEOTAPE PRACTICE SESSIONS

When you practice, videotape your sessions. Play the tape back and hit pause just before the shot is attempted. Analyze the court and player positions, and see what part of the court is open. Then hit play and see if you took the correct shot.

THREE-SHOT RALLIES

With your partner, serve, return, and then rekill. See if the shots go to the right place. Are you attempting the right shots? Player A serves the ball to player B who returns it. Player A then attempts a rekill if she has an offensive opportunity or a defensive shot if she does not.

POINTS-FOR-PROCESS GAME

Set game-by-game goals in practice for executing shots to the open court instead of winning the game. Put two pieces of masking tape on the front wall, one about four feet (1.2 meters) high and the other one foot (.3 meter) high. Aim between these two lines. Any shot hit there will rebound as a pass shot to the open court. This helps you improve your shot selection, and because killing the ball is not an option, only good shot selection will win. An added benefit of this game is conditioning. It is difficult physically to cover these passing shots. If you can hit good passes, consider the game a win, no matter the score. This will get you into the habit of concentrating on process, rather than outcome.

FREEZE DRILL

This drill requires a helpful and patient practice partner. Play a normal game, but when the rally ends, both players must freeze immediately. This helps each player determine if one took the correct shot and if the other is in position to return that shot. This is similar to videotaping a practice session, but instead of stopping a video, you stop live play. This gives you instant feedback on a shot you may not recall later. At first this drill feels strange because your impulse is to anticipate the next shot and be on the move, especially on the winning shot. Players may have to move back to the spots where they attempted the offensive shot and the defensive positioning.

Advanced Serves and Shots

Once you've become practiced in the fundamentals of racquetball and have played a few games against opponents, you will probably find yourself looking for ways to even further enhance your competitive game. The advanced serves and shots discussed in this last chapter should help you gain that extra edge.

Specialty Serves

Sometimes when you're up against a highly skilled opponent, the usual repertoire of serves just isn't enough to help you gain the upper hand. At these times, it helps to really mix it up and attempt to catch your opponent off guard. Try using some of the following serves to your advantage.

Inside-Out Drive Serve   This serve is hit closer to the body than other serves. The idea is to inside-out the ball as the great Yankee shortstop, Derek Jeter does. Jeter often drives balls to right field when pitchers try to jam him inside. In racquetball the server can hit the ball in an inside-out manner to create a different spin on the serve. Much like a knuckleball in baseball, the serve will spin and hit the side wall. This is very difficult to return. The serve also feels heavy on the racquet. A right-handed player hits this serve to the right (figure 12.1), and a left-handed player hits it to the left side. Sometimes the serve does not hit the side wall but achieves a balloon effect as it comes back a little higher and moves away from the receiver. When combined with a drive serve to the opposite side of the court off the same motion, the results are usually a weak return.

12.1   **Inside-out drive serve.**

Mannino Lob Serve   A variation of the Texas lob (high-to-low serve) is the Mannino lob, named after the man who invented it, Jason Mannino, the number one player in the world from 2002 to 2003. Mannino hits the lob at different angles but always uses the same approach (figure 12.2). Sometimes the serve has a straight trajectory from high to low into the back left side wall or back right side wall. Other times Mannino puts more air under the serve and gives it a higher trajectory, although the serve still ends in the same place. These different angles confuse the serve returner and make it difficult to return.

12.2   **Mannino lob.**

Different Lob Angles   In addition to using the Mannino lob, you can change the trajectories of lob serves by changing the hitting point on the serve. For example, you could hit down-to-up lobs. These are hit low and travel back high to the opponent. Strike the ball at about knee height, and follow through toward your chest. You can hit the same spot but lift the ball higher by following through over your head. From knee-high to a follow-through over your head produces a pop-fly lob (figure 12.3). This lob travels very high up on the front wall and rebounds deep into the backcourt. The high bounce makes this serve very difficult to attack.

12.3   **Pop-fly lob.**

Lob Approach The next variation in the lob serve is the approach. Instead of hitting a regular forehand stroke with a stiff wrist, approach the serve with an overhead motion. Instead of hitting down on the ball, hit a lob by opening the racket face toward the ceiling. This is a finesse serve and is not used much. It can be used with a Texas lob off the same motion, which makes it difficult to return aggressively. As with the Texas lob, the ball is struck head high or a little higher.

Walking Serve This serve is underused at all levels. The server hits the same serve, but instead of a traditional two-step approach, she uses a walking motion toward the right side or the left, which hides the ball momentarily from the receiver. The receiver's momentary confusion often results in easy scoring opportunities. The server can walk forward or backward to launch her serve.

The following are guidelines for the walking serve. The goal of the walking serve is to hide the ball from the receiver, so the natural direction to move is forward. A right-handed player playing a right-handed player should move backward. This hides the ball. If the right-handed player is playing a left-handed player, he should move to the right, or forward. The left-hander would move to the left if he is playing a right-handed player and toward the right, or backward, if he is playing another left-hander. Although this may sound complicated, these are the motions that best hide the ball from the receiver.

Advanced Z Serves Besides the low-to-high drive Z and the high-to-low serve mentioned in chapter 1, there is the snap Z. On this Z serve, the server snaps her wrist as hard as she can. The player slows the racket and snaps her wrist, which puts spin on the serve. If the serve can get to the side wall deep, the ball will kick off the side wall at a 45-degree angle. Also try the roll Z, which is hit softly by turning the wrist slightly upward just before contact. This lifts the serve slightly and keeps it chest high and hard to attack. This little lift in the middle of the swing also produces a tight angle into the corner. The Z serve travels across center court at an extreme angle that is hard to attack.

Lob Z Serve Angles To keep your opponent guessing, hit lob Z serves at two different angles. Hit one lob Z at a contact point waist to chest high. This gives a traditional look to the lob Z. Or hit the lob Z at a lower height; I call this *climbing the ladder*. The server strikes the ball lower, and it travels higher and more softly on the side wall and front wall, which causes a higher serve bounce in the backcourt. This lob Z is harder to return than the traditional lob Z.

More Serve Tips   Change the angle of the serve by using the different areas of the service zone. Serve from the left, to the right, and left of center. Switching areas creates different serve angles. Even when hitting the exact same serve as the previous one, it will be a different serve if it's hit from a different spot, and you will be more effective. Let's look at this a different way. If you have the basic selection of lob left and right, Z serve left and right, and drive serve left and right, those are six serves. Now use three different spots for each serve, and you have increased your repertoire to 18. To further increase the number of serves, vary the speed. Use the same motion as a drive serve, but hit a soft serve. This will throw your opponent's timing off. Use three different speeds for each serve, and now you have increased your number of serves to 54.

A serving tip that comes in handy if you play on different courts is: Let the court surface help determine your serve. A concrete or plaster court is very fast. The harder serves work better, and the softer serves have to be almost perfect. A player with less control can power the ball by someone with control on this surface. Also, remember that more balls will come off the back wall. The shot that will die in the corner on a panel wall will come off the back wall on a concrete court. Because the panel courts are slower, the slop lobs and soft Texas and Mannino lobs work well on this surface.

Specialty Shots for Extreme Situations

Sometimes extreme game situations require specialized shots. When the ball is difficult to reach, it may be necessary to take a desperation shot. Most of these specialty shots are low percentage, but if you play racquetball long enough, you will eventually see these shots.

Backhand Overhead Pinch Shot   This shot is hit off a high backhand ceiling ball. When the ball is over a player's head, his opponent will expect him to hit a ceiling ball because the ball is so high. Instead, hit a backhand that will end up in the opposite corner. This is called the *backhand overhead*. It is hit by aiming for the front right corner if the player is right-handed and the front left corner if the player is left-handed. The shot will be attempted from about 37 feet (11.3 meters) deep and shoulder high in the backcourt (figure 12.4). It is a very low-percentage shot, but some players have perfected this shot or a variation of it. This shot puts a lot of pressure

Backhand overhead pinch shot.

on a player who is used to hitting ceiling balls. Usually the ceiling ball is a safe shot, but not against the player who can execute the backhand overhead!

Front-Wall–Side-Wall Shot One high-percentage specialty shot is the front-wall–side-wall shot. This shot is made in the frontcourt when the ball is coming off the back wall to the frontcourt. The frontcourt player simply takes the shot and hits a front-wall side-wall shot at an extreme angle so that the ball dies immediately in the frontcourt. Once mastered, this shot is extremely effective and high percentage. This shot would only be used on front-wall shots where the ball is in an extreme setup position.

Around-the-Wall Ball Pass   Hit the around-the-wall ball pass during rallies. This shot can be effective at the top levels of the game during rallies. Instead of hitting the side wall high as a player would in a totally defensive around-the-wall ball, hit this shot about 8 to 10 feet (2.4–3 meters) high on the side wall. This catches a player by surprise and is difficult to cut off in the frontcourt. The high around-the-wall ball gives an opponent time to move into the frontcourt and cut it off. This shot works against players hitting around-the-wall balls. Cut off shots by moving into the frontcourt and catching balls hit off the back wall. The theory is that if the attacker moves up on a ball, she has better court position than the defensive player who just hit the shot. The player who just hit the ball into the back wall is out of position and unable to recover to move up on the ball. The short-hopping shot maker in the frontcourt has more room for error because of this.

Desperation Shot   If the ball gets past you, hit a desperation shot. Desperation shots are hit into the back wall to keep the ball in play, often because there is no other option. The trick is to keep the racket face open and hit at an upward angle. The ball does not have to be hit hard, only with an open racket face.

Diving Shots   Diving shots are hit when there are no other options. When diving, be careful not to injure your hands. Brace yourself with your off hand, and try to hit a defensive shot, if possible. Because of percentages, a defensive shot is preferred. The offensive shot must be perfect, but the defensive shot does not. An offensive attempt off your feet usually results in a ball left for an opponent in good court position waiting for the weak return. If you make a diving defensive shot, your opponent will have to move back to take the shot.

Behind-the-Back Shot   Use the behind-the-back shot when a ball is hit behind you. When there is not enough time to move your feet, simply put your racket arm behind your back, and stick the racket out with the face angled toward the ceiling (figure 12.5). This results in a behind-the-back ceiling ball. Not only does this shot save valuable time because it is almost impossible to move your feet

Behind-the-back shot.

fast enough, it is spectacular looking. "Flashy" is an adjective that comes to mind.

Between-the-Legs Shot This is a cousin of the behind-the-back shot. Most people are familiar with this shot because at least once in a broadcasted tennis tournament, a player runs to the backcourt and shoots a shot between his legs. Almost as flashy is the between-the-legs shot off the back wall in a racquetball match. Like the behind-the-back shot, the between-the-legs shot is hit when you have no other choice. This usually occurs when the ball hits a corner, takes a bad bounce, or comes right at the player going to the back wall. With your body facing the back wall, hit the ball between your legs. Like many of these specialty shots, this is desperation time!

Wrapping Up

It is a good idea to have goals in mind when playing games in practice. Many players play their practice matches with no object in mind other than winning. Winning is good, but practice exists for practice. "Just win, baby," which was the mantra of the Oakland Raiders, applies only to organized competition. Practice the shots that will make you more effective in competition, even if it means losing a few games. Don't forget to practice the serves you need to work on too. One way to focus on your practice time is to chart your practices. Keep a book of all of your practices and how you felt after and during them. Draw a happy face if it was a good practice and a sad face if it was a bad practice. Write little cues to help you hit good shots. For example, "Keep the elbow up" may be a cue to help you hit a better shot. Write this in the practice book so you can refer to the book when competition starts.

Doing everything in *Racquetball Fundamentals* will help you improve and become a better player. And no matter how good you get, you can continue to work on your physical fitness through weight training and cardiovascular workouts. Racquetball is largely an anaerobic activity, but a well-trained aerobic system replenishes the body during rest periods. The better your cardiovascular conditioning, the better you will perform on the racquetball court. Fitness clubs have someone on staff certified in physical fitness. Take advantage of these resources by employing a professional to examine your program and make changes and additions. A great player once said, "In order not to be concerned about fitness in competition, you had better be dealing with fitness in practice."

Racquetball is the greatest conditioning sport going. When you arrive at a health facility and report to the front desk, they often ask, "Are you playing racquetball, or are you working out?" I don't know about you, but I would rather play my calories away than work them away. So get off your boring stair steppers, bicycles, and other repetitive-motion machines, and get on the racquetball courts. Fitness with a stick is more fun than fitness with a slick machine! See you on the courts.

About the Writer

With more than 30 years of experience coaching athletes from the beginner to the elite levels, Jim Winterton is recognized as one of the best racquetball coaches in the world. He is director of the High Performance Racquetball Camp in Colorado Springs, Colorado, and has coached the U.S. national team for 12 years. During this time he has led his teams to five Tournaments of the Americas team crowns (1992, 1994, 1996, 1998, and 2002) and three first-place standings in the Pan American Games (1995, 1999, and  2003). Winterton also served a brief term as coach of the U.S. junior national team before accepting the position of head coach of the Mexican national team from 1999 to 2001.

He has been named Racquetball Coach of the Year by the United States Olympic Committee three times (1995, 1999, and 2003) and was a Racquetball Hall Of Fame inductee in 1999. Winterton is coaching clinician for the International Professional Racquetball Organization and is a certifying instructor for the American Professional Racquetball Organization. He also runs a racquetball program at Gold's Gym in Syracuse, New York. His coaching philosophy is simple: Practice makes perfect is not true; perfect practice makes perfect is true.

Winterton resides in Liverpool, New York.

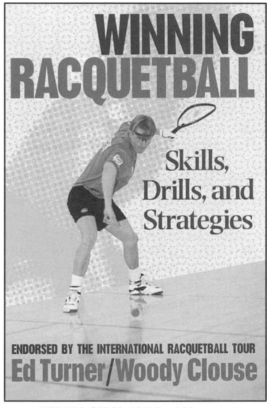